Stop Struggling In School

Wynford Dore

www.withzing.com

INTRODUCTION

Parents of children who struggle at school need hope, I remember all too vividly some very low moments. Sadly parents aren't getting much hope yet, despite important research breakthroughs that could give them great hope, if only it reached them. The current education system is not equipped to find the root cause of children's struggles so tends to write them off all too quickly and easily.

Here I share my story....the desperate need that my daughter, Susie had, the excitement of finding something that helped change her life and my struggle in the long journey to get this "hope" to the millions of families that need it right now.

Lots of credit and thanks goes to my daughter, Susie for forcing me to try and solve her challenges. I have had so much help along the way from wonderful professors and medical specialists who have given freely of their time and knowledge to make this possible.
My loyal team of co-workers have been awesome in turning what started as a stream of mad ideas into something structured and effective. I am eternally thankful to my soul-mate Ninka Mauritson who helps me persevere in the quest to reach millions of families.

Finally, if you know of other families with a struggling child - then please share what you glean from the book as giving real hope is a most precious gift.

Best wishes

Disclaimer

DEDICATION

This is dedicated to every Mum (Dad and Grandparent) who cares passionately about their children, who take responsibility for every aspect of their development and does NOT assume that schools can or will deal with every issue as it appears.

This will change the World.

CONTENTS

Stop Struggling In School

CHAPTER 1

CHANGING YOUR CHILD'S LIFE

"A capacity, and taste, for reading gives access to whatever has already been discovered by others."
Abraham Lincoln

Have you ever received negative emails from school about your "problem" child? Have you ever boiled over because of your child's frustratingly poor reading and homework hassle? Have you ever been angry because your child's clothes are all over the floor? That they do not clean up after themselves and frequently lose their gym clothes and bags? Have you been called into school for a meeting because your child forgets homework, disturbs the other pupils, loses emotional control or simply cannot focus? CONGRATULATIONS.

These are probably all signs of huge potential (that many well-behaved children with good grades have less of). When you have finished this book, you may even jump with joy if your child has all of these issues. You will finally understand why. You will know how to help your child to utilise the full potential of their brain with less of the current "problems" which makes school and family time stressful.

Did you know that more than enough research has been done showing exactly how schools could help reduce the struggles that children have? Problems like lack of focus, doing homework, self-esteem, depression, reading, reading comprehension, math, fidgeting and behaviour. All very familiar issues in schools everywhere. So why hasn't it been implemented? Does it cost too much? No! is it difficult to do? No! So why isn't every school doing it? the answer is I don't know. It beats me. And some of this research has been around for over a generation - and it's still being ignored.

Want to know what this amazing thing is? It's physical exercise - that's it, they must do more exercise. Eight years ago the US Department of Health and Human Science made this information available to education authorities - but hardly any of the methods described have been implemented in schools to this day. Why? And how much longer must children suffer when it is so easy to do something about it?

What's more the research makes clear that there is no downside to doing more exercise - nobody suffered in their learning because they spent more time doing physical exercise and a bit less doing the learning. And do you think the children love the idea - you bet they do.

I'm a dad of a daughter that struggled badly, so can you imagine how angry it makes me feel when I hear of children struggling when something easy that could be done that could help them - and it is being denied to them? So, I will share with you here what I have learnt from the last 20 years studying this subject - and it's in a form that you can easily give to your child ….. something that might make all the difference.

If schools aren't allowed to give your child what they need then it will be open minded warrior mums and dads that will provide it instead. Parents who care, who believe in their children's future and that are determined to find all the potential they have. I want to make that process easy for you.

If you want to access the US Department of Health and Human Services report, it's here;

https://www.cdc.gov/healthyyouth/health_and_academics/pdf/pa-pe_paper.pdf

It is my mission to give you the tools and the power needed to change your child's future. Sadly, so many children who struggle in childhood without this help end up struggling with depression, anxiety, suicidal tendencies, love and life in general. all because this secret link to the brain is currently hiding from parents.

In this book, I will reveal:

1. **The five ways in which experts entirely misunderstand children who struggle in school**

   No, they are not lazy.
   No, they are not unintelligent.
   No, they are not crazy.
   No, it is not bad genes or bad parenting.
   No, it is not for life.

2. **How you can test your child's symptoms to see if the cerebellum is the problem and solution for you.**

3. **The real root cause (that nobody is telling you about) and a neurological reset for:**

   Poor reading/dyslexia (nobody explains that it is usually about fixable eye tracking issues).

   Poor concentration/ADHD (nobody tells you the link to reduced listening and eye movement skills).

   Clumsiness/dyspraxia (nobody clarifies the link to balance and coordination and how to re-develop this).

   Forgetfulness (nobody tells you about the link to brain overload and how to deal with this by stimulating the inner ear).

4. **How you can become a warrior parent and help your child:**

By assisting your child in testing and resetting the brain, so that their mind will be ready for learning. You even get the chance to go back and consolidate previous (unsuccessful) attempts to learn that are STORED in the brain - waiting to be used. How awesome is that?

Your child is completely misunderstood and mistreated.

Here is the OLD way of dealing with a child like yours:

- Isolate the child in special classes.
- Focus on the PROBLEM.
- Criticise - treat them as if they are stupid or lazy.
- Practise, practise, practise reading, writing, etc.
- Worry and lose sleep.
- Give them a label.
- Assume that they are choosing not to learn.
- Develop coping strategies.
- Treat the symptoms.
- Quickly turn to medication.

Here is the NEW (my) way of dealing with a child like yours:

- Include, support and encourage - make them feel they are safe and BELONG – at school and at home.
- Focus on the POTENTIAL (these children often have more than other children).
- Understand and test the brain to find their potential.
- Commit to getting them to where they could have been, had they not had a problem.
- Focus on the root cause (the brain) and address it. Redevelop incomplete skill development with eye tracking and balance exercises to stimulate the brain within the brain (the cerebellum) which affects reading, emotional control, concentration and writing.

CHAPTER 2

MY DAUGHTER'S DYSLEXIA AND SUICIDE ATTEMPTS GAVE ME MY LIFE PURPOSE

*"Failure is simply the opportunity to begin again, this
time more intelligently"*
Henry Ford

One day back in the 1990's, the Wynford Dore I used to be was driving a sports car through the north of England. A two-hour drive away from home and utterly unaware of the disaster and the wakeup call ahead of me. If you had met me back then, you would have picked up the vibe of success. My private plane in the hanger at the airport, the yacht in the Mediterranean and my thriving business. I had revolutionised the fire protection industry as a respected, but disruptive, entrepreneur. What I did not share with anybody was the pain that always travelled with me. My daughter's depression, learning difficulties and anxiety had made her struggle terribly in school, and she was still tragically unhappy. It made me feel like a failure.

The Worst Phone Call - Little did I know that it was about to get even worse. A buzzing sound from the phone demanded attention. I slowed the car down. It was my daughter, and the desperate tone of her voice made my heart pound. She was talking about her older sister, my troubled, depressed child; "She's in the hospital. She has tried to take her life". As I asked, "what are the chances of her coming through?" the phone went dead. I was left in complete suspense for that agonising two-hour drive to the hospital. In the silence and panic that ensued, I weaved in and out of the cars that seemed to be going slower than ever in front of me on the motorway. I finally managed to navigate between them to get to my child. It was the loneliest, most painful two hours of my life, it felt like the end of the world. I was assuming the worst. In a frantic conversation with myself flitting between panic and inadequacy, I was asking "What else could I have done?"... "What didn't I think of trying?"..."Did I spend enough time with her?" ... "Did I try hard enough?" ... "Did I search enough for the right advisors, consultants, medical specialists, educational specialists?" I felt wholly wretched and guilty. No daughter deserves to feel so desperate at that beautiful, tender age.

My daughter's dreadful childhood and struggles in school.

As I was driving, my mind took me back to when my daughter was five. Why had she seemed normal up until then? Then why was it so impossible for her to learn basic things when she started school? My stomach churned as I recalled the memories of her suffering when teachers tried to teach her, and we all realised that nothing they taught was going in. She seemed bright, but she couldn't learn. She could not read. She could not write. Nothing was developing. To make it worse no one wanted to be her friend or have her on their sports team because she was so clumsy. She was taken out of classes to have special attention and still nothing was going in. She was lonely, sad and afraid. She did not seem to BELONG anywhere.

I remember the hopeless, helpless look on her face as she listened to my other three children exchange success stories of their results in spelling tests, exams and achievements in sport. She had nothing to share or celebrate.

I am used to making things happen in my businesses, so the pain of having a daughter that I loved dearly but was completely unable to help just made me feel numb and inadequate. Everyone was telling me; "There's nothing you can do about it."

Now I don't accept a "cannot do" attitude in life in general - and certainly not when it comes to my daughter. Then, as she went into her teens, she became worryingly depressed.

I felt like a dreadful father. I was desperate to learn why she was having difficulties, but I also got very irritated. I couldn't understand how my daughter, who seemed so bright, could be struggling in such a way.

No specialist's comments made much sense to me; nobody offered any solution or hope. She was merely told to; "Learn to live with it".

As I pulled up to the hospital, it was plain to see that she could no longer "live with it". She had just tried to end her life.

If my daughter survives…. (My promise to myself).

By the time I'd reached the hospital, I had made a decision. If by God's grace she survives this, I was going to change my life. I would sell my business and focus all my efforts on finding help and a solution that would transform her life. Little did I know that it would become part of a bigger plan to help - not only my daughter - but countless children with learning, behavioural and mood issues all over the world.

I hurried to find my daughter and family and, mercifully, the doctors gave me the good news that she was pulling through. I cannot describe my feeling of relief - those who saw my tears had some sense of how great it was.

My life had been changed by the decision I had taken in the harrowing drive to the hospital. The Wynford Dore I used to be was no more. This was a wake-up call. I went home to start my research - but where was I to start? I quickly concluded that I HAD to find a vital link that everybody had missed and then hunt for experts that understood whatever that missing link was. It felt like more of a challenge than searching for a needle in a haystack…at least then you know what you are searching for and you stand a chance. At this point, I had no clue.

A synchronistic sign from the universe.

My first clue was precisely the breakthrough I had been looking for. It felt like a sign from the Universe. I was impatiently flipping through books in the airport in Hong Kong. I was visiting my office there; run by my friend, Charlie. I wanted to give him a book by John Gray – Men Are From Mars, Women Are From Venus but my attention was taken away by another cover. It was like this other book was calling me. It was about part of the brain called the cerebellum and its surprising role in learning and child development.

As I carried the book in a plastic bag on board the flight, I still had no clue that I was moving closer to my life purpose and that this book would lead me to my daughter's recovery. This was the first step on a journey to find the secret way of resetting the brain so that children who struggle can live and learn more effortlessly.

My second wake-up call.

As I started my 13-hour flight, I took a sleeping tablet and casually picked up the book, thinking I'd read a few pages and fall asleep. Within five pages, I was more wide awake than ever before. This was my second wake-up call. On the flight, I read it from cover to cover. The very next day I made arrangements to meet the author who helpfully pointed me to even more exciting research. The research showing a link between a specific area in the brain and learning difficulties. It was important research that wasn't reaching the people that desperately needed it.

It was the flash of hope I needed, and it put my life and my research journey into overdrive.

Everything I have learnt in this book, including the science behind it, I will share with you in chapter four: *The truth that has been hidden from you.*

The disruptive entrepreneur in me went wild.

I'm not used to hanging around when there are things to do. When running a previous project for fire-resistant paint, within six months of starting I had created the best product of its type in the world. This new project was focused on helping my daughter and needed even faster progress as I lived in dread of getting another phone call.

Within weeks I had found the professors who could steer this breakthrough with cutting-edge science. One was (and still is) at Harvard and the other in the UK. NASA had developed a vital device to measure some fundamental brain skills - I sent one of my researchers to the US to buy it. A team of doctors and other experts were assembled, all with a passion to help and, as this was breakthrough science a completely open mind.

The solution was not going to be found in the conventional areas of study; we needed to think outside the box.

Fortunately, this team loved this approach as they knew that problems like this were getting worse and worse – and no one was finding the solution. Their sleeves were rolled up ready for action.

The clinics - screams of joy.

We were getting ready for our first trials, the clinic was opened, and I looked for parents of children that were struggling. Within days there was a queue of parents, all saying the same thing, that there is no hope or help out there for my child. These parents were prepared to try something entirely different to free their children from the limitations that nobody understood. We were off .... piecing together research like a giant jigsaw puzzle. Every day we'd find another piece that fits confirming that there was hope. The hope that had been missed by the mainstream. I'll never forget those early weeks, the frequent screams of delight that echoed around the office as we discovered more and more research that helped us to get closer to the results we craved.

Missing link #1 - eye tracking

To help my daughter I was looking in medical areas that many others had overlooked. I was talking to researchers from disciplines that had never considered that they could help increase a child's ability to learn. The eye tracking equipment we bought showed parents precisely what happens when their child tries to read. They'd make gasps of surprise as they watched their child's eyes jumping around on the big screen instead of smoothly following the line of the book they were trying to read. Parents wanted to know why nobody had told them that this was their child's issue before. For us to see their problem so clearly gave us a very specific challenge to focus on - we must improve their eye tracking to provide them with a chance of reading easily.

It felt like a war zone.

When there is a war raging people's minds are much more focused than usual and with that mind-set, scientific breakthroughs are far more common. For me, saving my daughter was a war and everyone in the research team felt the urgency, every day mattered. When the trials started, we collected every bit of research data and analysed it every day. Who is making progress? What is causing it? If we do more of this and less of that, what happens? It was a structured frenzy with constant surprises and only a few disappointments.

Our first result was a shock because it wasn't what we expected. We were trying hard to help children read easier and better. I believed this was the root of my daughter's troubles (at this point we had no clue that so many symptoms that children struggle with actually have the same common cause). So we were looking for improvements in reading. We didn't expect any gains for a few months, but within 2-3 weeks parents were saying things like "reading hasn't improved yet, but their confidence is definitely increasing".

A massive breakthrough.

This happened frequently, and each time the research team would look at each other and ask, "What is going on?" We hadn't a clue - and it was some time before we did work out what was actually happening. Finally we realised that we were improving the automaticity of a number of crucial skills in the brain. We were trying to help reading by stimulating the cerebellum (brain within the brain), in the hope that eye tracking and other skills needed for reading would improve. Instead, by accident (I wish I could say by design but I can't take credit for that), we were helping a far wider set of skills to develop, among them were verbal and auditory processing, the very skills needed for communication. As a result, children were becoming more of a natural at listening and speaking. They were growing more confident and gaining more friends. What a great surprise.

It wasn't long before we got the news we were waiting for, that reading was also getting easier too. Can you imagine the sense of relief? My daughter was 27 at this time, and we wondered whether we'd have to try teaching her again, if and when we could get her eye tracking issues sorted. She made rapid progress in reading - so quick that we couldn't understand how or why. She seemed to have retained what she had been taught 20 years earlier and was no able to use it. How is that possible? It would be years before we knew the answer to that question, but our relief was immediate. Within three months she was starting to read. Then came the next shock. Her handwriting began to improve too. And so it went on, we kept having surprises, and more and more people started hearing about our success.

The clinic was getting busier and busier, parents kept telling others, and we became inundated. All the while we collected research data so we could improve and fine tune our methodology.

The press discovered us.

Then the media heard what we were achieving and they turned up in droves. They spoke to parents and children, they checked with teachers. What was too good to be true was actually happening. Trevor McDonald, a famous documentary maker in the UK, asked if they could make a documentary. I said they could, so they brought along two children and an adult to start the course. I was worried - what if they were filmed but weren't actually doing the daily exercises that we asked them to do for 10 minutes a day for six months? This would be a disaster for us. These were people that at the time didn't believe in what we were doing, they knew nothing of my track record in researching new products - they didn't need to believe in the science but they did have to comply with the programme …. our reputation was on the line.

I needn't have worried. When the TV production team saw their eye tracking results on the screen, they knew we were onto something and so it wasn't long before they saw excellent results, as did the TV cameras. They brought along an adult, he was a delightful dad, very shy but he couldn't read. He also had a poor memory for names and, therefore, had low confidence. All of that changed during the six months that he completed our course and his wonderful progress was followed by the TV cameras.

So far so good in the war!
The results we had continued to get better and better. By this time many franchisees had approached us to open clinics in several countries, and all had (unsurprisingly) the same wonderful results.

Then the attacks started ….

The media told the story honestly as they could see for themselves that the results were so undeniable.

But sadly, after a year or so, a few attacks started to happen. The attacks weren't coming from parents, but from academics connected to the traditional approaches to learning difficulties. Some were the very researchers whose methods have left more and more parents facing deeply challenging issues in these children. These had been the significant influencers during the decades when these problems have only got worse and worse - and they attacked us of all people. I had expected that altruism would have led them to talk to us and to the academics who advised us.

I was spending millions on research, never taking a cent back, working 16-hour days to help my own daughter and thousands of others. We collected enormous amounts of scientific data from over 40,000 children and adults. We knew exactly what we were doing and achieving. Even more importantly, the families we helped really appreciated what we achieved for them.

From the start, I had subsidised every single client, including clients in those franchisees in other countries. Not being Bill Gates, I am not able to do that for all of the millions of people that need this help. Funding the clinics and the research while subsidising so many who wanted aid became harder and harder.

The devastating end of the first part of the journey.

Without those attacks, we could have taken it around the world and reached millions, but it wasn't to be. The attacks meant that fewer were coming to the clinics. Led by people that evidently did not care about the children nor the science. I was going to run out of money, and my body was suffering - many years of working long days were taking their toll.

I had failed. I couldn't keep all the clinics open, so many clinics had to close. Disaster for those families we still had not helped, and a smirk on the face of those that attacked me. They thought that they had won the day for their own reputation and revenue.

My job for the next few months was to help these families that had not finished their course so they didn't lose out. I succeeded in the UK, but in other countries run by franchisees, it was not always possible. I spent vast amounts of money trying to help as many as possible but was not able to access the databases to get to everyone. I was devastated, I had let down some of the very families I wanted to help.

You can imagine the anger I felt towards the critics.

How could they be so cruel, so unscientific even? A high proportion of people that commit suicide have learning issues of one sort or another, and now another generation has suffered, and some have died, needlessly. I see those critics as having a lot to answer for.

The remaining clinics were sold to a company that wanted to run them, and I retired exhausted, devastated and embarrassed. Despite the fact that a large number of the families I had helped keep in touch and said wonderful things, but I was still a failure in my eyes.

For 18 months I couldn't even think about a struggling child or my life purpose. I blanked it out of my mind.

My eureka moment.

Then I woke one day and instantly knew what I had to do. Eureka! I had a new vision and it was that I was to go about my life purpose in a totally different way. The children that were struggling seemed to be so much brighter than the average kids, the opposite of how they had been regarded. So I must not try and help "learning difficulties". Instead, I must focus on "finding potential" and improving their actual skills.

So much more research had appeared from universities during the last few years adding weight to what we had been doing and opening up even more possibilities. Technology had moved on. My vision now became the possibility that I could get help to families without them being hassled by visiting clinics or seeing doctors. They would develop their key skills and be transformed without leaving home, by simply following programmes on their computer or smartphone.

They would be able to do quick online tests and measure their real potential, and this will give them real hope. They'll be able to measure the progress of their brain development as they go. I was so excited by this possibility I couldn't wait to get started again in this new direction.

Suddenly, the disappointment of what I had seen as a failure had taken on a new perspective. My new vision would enable far more families around the globe to access this fantastic breakthrough.

With the help of those families who care, we will win this war and get help to the millions that need it.

CHAPTER 3

YOUR CHILD HAS BEEN COMPLETELY MISUNDERSTOOD

"The old believe everything, the middle-aged suspect everything, the young know everything."
Oscar Wilde

I once watched a diabetic person in an acute emergency. She was pulled over by the police because it looked like she was driving drunk. She was swearing, slurring and swaying as everyone stepped away in disgust - judging her. Until they realised that she was in trouble and needed treatment for her diabetes. She needed understanding, but she was judged and rejected because people ASSUMED she was something she wasn't. The misunderstanding could have ruined (or ended) her life.

What if your child who struggles with reading, writing, emotional control, behaviour and concentration is just as misunderstood as that person with diabetes? What if your child's life is currently in danger of being ruined by people who reject and judge them because they ASSUME that their issues are psychological and psychiatric when, in reality, their problems are neurological?

What if your child needs UNDERSTANDING and the right TREATMENT, brain-stimulating exercises so that they behave, learn and focus like everybody else. Just like the person with diabetes acted completely normally after receiving the right treatment?

In the medical system, doctors and ambulance personnel are trained to tell the difference between a drunk and a person with diabetes.

Understandably, in schools, the experts are educationalists. They are not trained to tell the difference between a psychological problem and a neurological problem. That is why your child is struggling and not getting the help they need. This is why you need to be the neurological rescue team for your child.

The five ways some experts misunderstand your struggling child.

Myth #1 - "Slow learners are unintelligent."
Why they misunderstand:
Teachers (and parents) tend to misunderstand those children that can't retain information, can't read very much, can't write very much, and score poorly in exams. In a teacher's world, this usually means low intelligence.

Why is this so wrong.
First of all, exams don't measure all types of intelligence. A lot of exams only measure the ability to regurgitate information. Creativity is an intelligence and children with it question conventional systems. Creativity doesn't like being put in boxes and, instead, thinks outside of them. Secondly, your child is probably struggling to take in information when reading because of eye movement issues and the inability to process. This can lead to working memory overload (more on this in the next chapter). If a child cannot concentrate because of neurological problems (that often can be addressed easily) they are not able to even retain and regurgitate.

It causes so much misunderstanding. The majority of children that struggle at school are wrongly accused of being unintelligent, yet the opposite is often true. Parents often SENSE the bright brain in their child and don´t understand why schools fail to find the obvious potential. The answer is simple. Teachers are taught little if anything about this science that has been hidden from everyone. We will get to this later.

Just be assured that your child may well have great ideas even though they can't express them yet in writing. You may sometimes wonder about this if you ever see your child communicate in an adult way that belies their years.

So, what is the truth?

The more intellect you have, hidden or not, the more wiring is needed in the brain. The ideas, thoughts and concepts that a creative brain produces is somewhat like a powerful fire hose; you can't hold back the flow. If your child doesn't write much or is maybe a bit shy about getting complex thoughts out in words, then you may not see their stream of ideas, but it doesn't mean that they're not there. They have more than one challenge. Firstly, people often don't see their intelligence; they don't show it in the traditional way. Secondly, the super flow of ideas needs huge processing capacity, lots of mental capacity to process all of that information. They may have a normal amount of processing capacity, but not enough to cope with a fire hydrant. There just isn't enough thinking brain space to deal with it. That's why a child can get a sense of overwhelming overload and frustration. They don't choose to be frustrated, it happens and makes them feel terrible, misunderstood and helpless.

Some of the brightest people in the world have dropped out from school and college and shown their genius later on in life. That doesn't mean that every child that's struggling in school is a genius. However, the irony is that the brighter you are, the more likely that it is that you will experience struggles in fundamental things like reading, concentration, and writing.

If reading and listening are the main two ways in which you take in information at school, and both are somewhat impaired, then you will not be retaining much information. Often those children are the ones that go on to learn by themselves, they learn by doing, and they work things out in their own unique way. That is true intelligence.

How this misunderstanding affects your child.

A bright child that is criticised, taken out of class and forced to read out loud is MISUNDERSTOOD, and they know it. It affects their confidence, and it can ruin their school life, exams and social life. Everyone sees the PROBLEM instead of their bright brain and the massive potential in your child. If you don't do something about this it will affect their life and happiness in adulthood as well.

Myth #2 - "Children that struggle in school are lazy" - what's the truth?

Why they are misunderstood:

These children often appear slow. So teachers see them taking forever to do simple things like reading, writing or doing maths. They interpret this as laziness.

Why is this so wrong?

It always hurts me to hear children described as lazy, and I take every opportunity to correct whoever I hear say it. Children who struggle do so because they have not fully developed and automated the most important processes in their brain, so they're having to use an extra mental process and "think" about them. This extra process is both slow and hard. It's a bit like the old days before the internet, instead of using email and clicking "send" so that the information is transmitted instantly, their brain is painfully slow, rather like waiting for the postman. It takes forever to get information there. Sometimes people say; "you can see the cogs whirring". Whenever your child has to "think about something", it's hard work. Whether it's reading, concentration, writing or playing sports, it's only easy and fun when it's mentally effortless. And it's only effortless when the wiring in the brain to perform that skill has been fully developed.

So, what is the truth?

Calling a child lazy is cruel when they are doing their best with the mental limitations they currently have. In this book, you will learn how the fully automatic functions in the brain take place in our brain's cortex. Where the speed of processing is up to a million times faster than in our "thinking brain". We'll also learn how processing skills in the cortex will make life so much easier as you won't have to "think" so much.

How does this misunderstanding affect your child?

No one has explained to them that they were born that way and so they know no different. Often they assume that everyone's brain is the same, so they are puzzled, confused and sometimes even scared. Being so completely misunderstood is very traumatic for a child.

Myth #3 - "Children that struggle at school have inherited bad genes from their parents."

Why do they misunderstand?

A struggling child is often misunderstood and so are their parents. When a child refuses to sit still, runs away from school, does not do homework, forgets gym clothes or does not read as they are told to, some assume that there is something wrong with their genes.

Why is this so wrong?

Parents often worry about this, understandably, but I've not seen any evidence to suggest that this is true. In fact, often the opposite is true. Some children inherit an extraordinary brain from very intelligent parents.

What is the truth?

So what is happening? Well, it's like that fire hose again. If your children have a huge stream of ideas, they need the rest of their brain's capacity (neurology) to be developed to a higher than average degree. So if you're a parent with a child that's struggling, stop blaming yourself. The truth is almost certainly the opposite of what you believe.

Myth #4 - "Parents are doing a bad job"
Why are they misunderstanding this?

Again, with a child who seems lazy, slow or out of control, some teachers seem to think that these children are spoilt and need discipline, they need "boundaries". So the parents are blamed for "creating a monster".

Why is this so wrong?

This is more about neurology, less about child psychology. Many parents have been told that the reason that their child is having challenges at school is due to bad parenting, but they may well have other children who have received the same nurturing and are doing perfectly fine at school. Great parents, same strategy, different results. The real reason? The struggling child´s neurological development.

What is the truth?

A powerful brain moves fast. Some children are born with such powerful brains that when developing they can jump important developmental phases. This delays the completion of some aspects of development and affects essential skills, mood, personality, the ability to learn and to control emotions. What is needed is more vestibular stimulation (I will come to what and how in the next chapters). What is not useful is "blaming" or "shaming" the parents.

How does this misunderstanding affect your child?

I want to emphasise that persistently misunderstanding a child, calling them all the things that we have just covered, lazy, slow, unintelligent, can be very traumatic for the child. They were born that way and they don't know how to be any different.

When a child sees that their siblings are doing well and achieving in school, it confuses them more. No one has been able to explain to them why they are the way they are, and the trauma of persistent misunderstanding can compound any emotional problems they have.

Myth #5 "It is for life - learn how to live with it."
Why they misunderstand.

Experts tend to be specialised in their own field of expertise. So for instance, educationalists do not look into the field of nutrition or neurology. They learn to address learning and behavioural issues from an educational stand point which often means: isolate the child, offer coping strategies, give special education facilities or send the child to a doctor, psychologist or psychiatrist.

Why is this often wrong?

This course of action is sometimes necessary because the help they need is pressing and can't wait. Sadly however, this course of action is not always "thought through" thoroughly, and the child is often summarily given a label. But, what if that child is labelled for life and subsequently the symptoms disappear? Did that child even deserve the label in the first place? I find this very problematic. Never label a child before key brain skills, (eye tracking, visual and auditory processing, balance and coordination etc.) have been thoroughly examined. I will tell you all about how and where this happens in the following chapters.

What is the truth?

The truth is probably very different to what you have been told. The fact is that your child's symptoms could be just temporary, caused by lack of vestibular stimulation in early childhood, lack of eye tracking skills and lack of auditory processing skills. I believe that you can address and redevelop these skills, and I have written this book to explain to you how.

How does this misunderstanding affect your child?

If a child only meets experts who tell the child to "live with these limitations", then the struggles will probably last for life. If the root causes are not addressed and solved, then the lack of emotional control, learning skills, working memory capacity and social skills are likely to lead to many problems when the child grows up. Statistically, these neurological issues are linked to increased risk of depression, anxiety, addictions and suicidal tendencies. This is why you must become the expert your child doesn't have in school or the educational system.

If you address the root cause and the symptoms disappear - did the child even need a label in the first place?

I worry about how glibly labels are handed out sometimes and how they can stigmatise your child, adding to the misunderstanding that surrounds them. I also want to offer you hope. Instead of worry and focusing on problems, we should celebrate the symptoms as a hint link that there could be the potential of a big, powerful brain. Instead of giving it a sticker for life, we should give the child hope and encouragement to fine the genius and potential hidden behind the symptoms.

They say "ADHD" - I say "poor eye tracking, listening skills and working memory overload". Albert Einstein, Walt Disney and John F. Kennedy had symptoms that today would justify a label. Likewise Richard Branson, Justin Timberlake, Jim Carrey, and Michael Jordan. Some of the most brilliant brains dropped out of school because they were misunderstood. The link between genius and learning challenges is evident. Are children who struggle with reading, writing, concentration and emotional control welcomed into the group of genius innovators of this world? Do we celebrate and start developing their potential to become the next Richard Branson? No. We call parents into school meetings, send worried emails, take them out of class or send them to the doctor.

About one in five children show distinct signs of struggling with concentration. Some of them get a label or diagnosis. These numbers are increasing year, after year, after year. What's going wrong?

My partner's son had this issue.

My partner's youngest son is extremely bright however he was kicked out of four different schools in Denmark. He went through school until year eight without learning. He couldn't sit still. His mom had emails from schools all the time about how he was a bad influence on others and how he couldn't concentrate. He never did his homework; he was a problem child. He would never be able to pass exams because he lacked the foundational work, teachers said. That was then. Now he's doing well, passing his exams and getting rewarded for his behaviour, all this in a foreign language in a foreign country. So how did he get into trouble before? What is the reason behind this previous behaviour? What's created the transformation?

Every year in recent years the number of children diagnosed has increased. What's happening? The classic symptoms of ADHD are poor concentration, often poor behaviour, impulsivity and hyperactivity. All of these symptoms are determined by the effectiveness of the executive function, the "boss" of the brain. This is the area at the front of the brain where the working memory is located; it is an area that we improve by developing critical skills.

It is an area that can be developed by doing specific physical exercises that stimulate the vestibular system.

The brain/body connection, not the reading and writing, itself that needs special attention.

In a perfect world, these children would be handed a personalised physical exercise programme instead of more discipline or behavioural interventions. WHY do we STILL treat the symptoms instead of the cause?

Do these children have a problem with fundamental intelligence? No. Not according to the research I have pieced together in this book. Their problem is the under development in brain/body connections.

The connection with reading and writing issues.

Children labelled with "ADHD" often, but not always, have problems with reading and writing as well as concentration. Yet, someone has chosen to give them the label ADHD rather than dyslexia - and there are often arguments between specialists about the diagnosis of individual children. From what we now know about the cause of these conditions, the very way that labels are given to children must be re-thought and re-defined.

Root cause: Poor listening skills.

Children labelled with dyslexia and with ADHD often show signs of an auditory processing (listening) issue. This is a skill that's developed (or sometimes not) by the cerebellum. When it is not fully developed, it means when they are trying to listen, that they have to work extremely hard. They need to go through an extra mental process to convert what they hear into words they understand. This is not just difficult; it's exhausting for them. They're often accused of being lazy as if they are choosing not to concentrate. But concentration is hard work for them, these children need sympathy and understanding. A child with auditory processing issues does as much exhausting mental work concentrating for just a few minutes as other children in the class will do in the whole school day.

It is about the brain, not the behaviour.

These children have to use their thinking brain too much for far too many everyday tasks. The thinking brain gets so overloaded every day, that they don't have the mental speed and capacity to take in things they are taught, so they turn into concepts they understand. They jump from activity to activity in a disruptive, uncontrolled way.

They aren't choosing to behave like that; they are wired to.

The missing link in behavioural therapy.

Who would have thought that brain overload may be behind many of the issues we look to therapists to help solve? The missing link is the incomplete development of the cerebellum. The incomplete development shows up as poor concentration, poor focus on school and homework, tantrums, aggressive behaviour and lack of emotional control. To sum it up, these children are not stupid, crazy or any such thing.

The cerebellum has not finished the work of developing fundamental skills. I'm talking about the many thousands of balance, visual, verbal and other crucial mental processing tasks we take for granted, things that just "happen" without us thinking. Researchers say that typically one in six of these brain tasks never get perfectly wired and, depending on which particular skills that miss out, it can be enough to overload the thinking brain. Unless all the everyday mental processes a child needs are so hardwired that they become automatic, effortless, and instant, the poor old thinking brain has to finish off the processing and it's not good at the job.

The thinking brain is a very busy area of the brain, it's like the RAM of your computer, and when it gets overloaded, it is goodbye to concentration and control of your impulses or emotions. All sorts of things are going wrong.

So a child with ADHD/ADD symptoms is actually mentally exhausted. Not crazy. Their thinking brain is so full that they don't have enough mental capacity to make good decisions, control their impulsivity or maintain focus. These are children that are dreadfully misunderstood, and, the worse they behave, the more misunderstood they are.

Don't let systems steal your hope.

So often when these children are examined from a psychiatric or psychological standpoint, they tend to be stigmatised, given labels, maybe put into a special needs class. Both child and parents are told that this is something you may need to cope with for life. This is not necessarily true and unfair to both child and parents.

All expectation of hope is taken away, and there's been no attempt to identify any hidden potential or, even worse, there's been no check to see if the symptoms are solvable.

In the family situation, you've maybe got a child that's been labelled by the school as a naughty and troublesome child. At home, the child is often very disruptive also, probably not very organised, probably impossible to structure and always forgetting things; this can be a difficult situation. The child is misunderstood. The child is not choosing to behave like this at school or home, yet everyone treats them as if they are. They are hardwired to behave in this way, and they need understanding.

For such children, it's really important that you take their nutritional needs seriously. Children like this are very sensitive to the kind of foods they eat. There's plenty of research out there that you can look up that will point you to how gluten, dairy, sugar and additives in food can sometimes have a very significant impact, do check it out.

They say dyslexia - I say poor eye tracking skills.

I wish someone had told me this when my daughter was labelled "dyslexic". If I could, I would stand on a box and shout out this hidden truth to every parent of a child with this label.

"Eye tracking issues are the biggest cause of poor reading."

It is wrong to assume that your child is unintelligent because they can't (yet) read well. So, why can't your child read as well as others of the same age? The explanation is usually so simple that you will find it hard to believe. So is the potential solution. This might even make you angry. It has to do with the way your child's eyes take in information. Virtually all of the 1000's of children I've seen with reading problems have difficulties with eye tracking, the ability to smoothly use their vision to take in words from the page. The process is not fully developed for them, so their eyes are jumping around instead of moving effortlessly from letter to letter. When your child looks at a word in a book, their eyes jump about. The letters end up in a scrambled order. Sometimes their eye is even moving the WRONG way so that the letters actually enter the brain backwards. What a nightmare. This challenged brain has to unscramble those letters and put them in the correct order. That's hard work.

How it feels to be your struggling child.

Then, after the slow and painful process of working out what the word might be, the brain has to store the word somewhere so that the child can move on to the next word in the sentence.

Where do they store it? In the thinking brain - the slow, inefficient part of the brain. That very busy place. The thinking brain is the bit of memory we use to deal with everything we're doing right now. It's where we rationalise things and think them through, make decisions and keep lists in our mind. Our conscious thoughts all happens there. WOW! The place is full already, and now your child has to use it to hold the words as they struggle to read them.

So, the next word comes along, and again the letters are all over the place, some even backwards and the whole process starts all over. By the time others would have read and finished the chapter, this child is still struggling to store the first few words.

Meanwhile, some teachers start demanding more focus, harder work or effort. So unfair on the child.

So the first words read are pushed out of the thinking brain. Forgotten. This is such an exhausting process for them and at the end of the sentence, they discover that most of the words have been forgotten, and it is necessary to reread the whole sentence.

By this time the child has not taken in much, if anything, and you may see their eyes watering with tiredness because of the effort. Nobody seems to understand why it is so impossible for them.

This child is working ten times harder than everybody else and deserves a medal. Instead, they get a label and no help. I want to give you an opportunity to offer the support your child deserves.

Can you see how cruel it is when children are told that they must try harder, must focus and must concentrate? I remember when my own daughter was trying to read, and I assumed that she just wasn't trying hard enough. I was ignorant about the issues she faced. If only I had realised then just how impossible it was for her, I'd have been far, far more sympathetic.

They say dyspraxia - I say incomplete cerebellar development.

Dyspraxia is a label used to describe children that are particularly clumsy. They bump into things, they fall over, and when you see them walk, you can see that there is very little automaticity in the coordination of their movements. Often their legs and arms are dangling about. Their neck may even be bowed a bit as they're not holding it up straight. On the sports field, their clumsiness makes it hard to catch, throw or kick balls.

The cerebellum needs to finish a job.

What's really going on? Again, the cerebellum has not completed development of the coordination of their limbs and balance. So, when this child moves around, the thinking brain (the good old busy place from previous pages) is very involved in the process. Not good. Remember when you learned how to ride a bike before it became automatic? The feeling of dyspraxia is best explained by comparing it to having to relearn how to ride a bike every time you get on one. You have to think about every move. Balance, coordination, nothing is automatic. You are clumsy, insecure, wobbly and bump into things or fall of. Just like when you were practicing on your bike, the brain needs to hardwire and automatize balance, coordination and steering. When the job is done, it is effortless and you don't have to think about it. With dyspraxia, it's as if the brain is sending weak, vague and imprecise signals to the muscles.

This child needs help with redeveloping and hardwiring the skills of movement, balance and coordination, NOT a label.

I will show you how in upcoming chapters. When balance and co-ordination are automatic, the thinking brain doesn't need to get involved. They move automatically without any clumsiness. The computer programme that the cerebellum has created takes over, so everything is consistent, effortless, and they naturally balance, move about and can play a sport with greater confidence if they wish too.

The link to reading.

Many children with the label dyspraxia also suffer from reading issues. Because clumsiness is the most obvious issue, that's the label that they've been given. Why, oh why don't experts look at all of these children holistically and realise that they have several symptoms, and the root cause of each is the development of the cerebellum? When this becomes routine practice more will understand that there is something can be done about them. Finally, we can look forward to reducing, or maybe eliminating the number of children that are labelled.

They say autism is genetic - I say "what if it is neurological?"

My heart goes out to families that have an autistic child. The anguish of living with a child struggling with so many issues is just unthinkable. There is pressure on that family from all sides. It's made worse because no one is able to explain what these children are struggling with fully. There are endless arguments and disagreements between experts about what autism is and even more debates about an individual's diagnosis.

But there's pressure from the outside too. Some have the absurd notion that children with autism and misbehave must have had bad parenting. This could not be further from the truth. When an autistic child goes to school, most teachers understandably can't cope. They don't have the training or the tools to understand or deal with a child that has so many issues.

My partner's son.

In the case of my partner's eldest son, his diagnosis was infantile autism; he could not function normally. His early years were traumatic both for him and for his family as they tried to make him behave in a normal fashion. This proved to be impossible. He would rather lie on the floor and scream than respond to exhortations from his parents.

When he was at school, learning proved impossible and that was the sad pattern of events until he was 16.
During those early years, his parents worked very hard to give him the best nutrition possible and to detoxify his body from harmful chemicals. They also gave him crude but effective sensory stimulation activities that started to increase his brain's ability to acquire fundamental skills. He lost many of the symptoms of autism. But still, at the age of 16, he'd made little progress in his academic learning. His years in the grip of the severe symptoms made him fall behind; he'd missed out on crucial phases of development such as crawling, developing the ability to interact socially and how to have physical contact with others naturally. This affected his chances of having a good education and living as a typical adult.

When I met his mom, he was 16. After testing his brain strengths and weaknesses, I started him on a brain stimulation programme personalised for his needs.

Passing exams in a foreign country after having learned nothing for nine years.

To everyone's amazement in less than one year, he was able to finish his final exams in his native country, Denmark. Since then, he has gone on to do college courses to develop the music skills which he is so brilliant at. Now he's started a Level III course, equivalent to the first year of a university degree -

this is no ordinary transformation. It would be wrong to promise that this level of change is likely to happen in every similar case. But his story is not unique and changes like this happen more and more.

Let's focus on hope.

His story should bring great hope to those with autistic children. In this chapter, I have no intention of going into the debate about labelling, whether is it appropriate or not. I've no intention of joining the discussion about what causes autistic symptoms. These topics are a hotbed of fierce discussion the world over. My experience, and what parents can do about these challenges, is what I will stick to right now.

The general assumption is that there is something fundamentally wrong with the brain. I'm not going to spend the time to debate or argue that. My focus is what I can DO about it that will have a positive impact. Many researchers need to examine and understand "why" something is happening. I start at the other end. I want to "solve" the problem and then wonder why it happened in the first place.

In my work with children with autistic symptoms, I have focused on correcting the cause of those symptoms where possible. They display a whole series of areas of reduced skill development. Some, but not all, struggle with reading, while some are actually brilliant at reading, some can't read at all. Most have issues with social skill development. They can't easily read facial expressions, body language or develop sensitivity to other people's feelings. This hampers their ability to develop friendships and have a full life. Some are physically clumsy; some aren't, others have emotional control issues; a few don't.

They simply lack skill development.

I perceive all of the challenges that they have as inadequate or incomplete skill development. I've used my knowledge of the brain-body connection to develop natural ways of improving these skills, and the results have been very remarkable. When you remove skill limitations, the child is transformed, they now stand a chance of a more full and happy life, just what their parents crave for.

Let's focus our attention on solving the practical, neurological issues these children face and not waste time and emotional energy on endless debates and arguments.

The challenges of autism and Asperger's syndrome are so critical that it deserves the focus of another book. If the subject is of interest to you, watch this space.

Why some autistic children are picky eaters.

Increasingly, research is showing us the importance of the link between the gut and the brain. There's lots of debate about whether what we put into the body and what ends up in the gut affects the brain, or whether what how we develop of the brain affects the gut. I strongly suspect both are partly correct. Many of these children are very picky eaters. They won't consider eating certain foods that parents know are healthy, and they insist on having other foods that are unhealthy. This exacerbates their problems, and parents' exasperation is understandable when they face such issues.

I've observed many children who have used vestibular stimulation programmes starting to choose healthier food. Parents look at them puzzled when they no longer have to force them to eat their veggies. They just seem to want to. How and why this happens we've not yet worked out, but the fact it happens in many cases is really encouraging.

They say anxiety - I say lack of vestibular stimulation.

When my daughter was struggling with learning, I didn't realise that at least 50% of children who have difficulties like her develop problems with control of their emotions, depression, anxiety and/or panic attacks. Some, as in the case of my daughter, have suicidal tendencies. No one seems to talk about this connection. When my daughter tried to take her life, it became critical to me, and I'm sure it will become increasingly so to every parent that has a child struggling at school.

In the US 1 in every 13 children will have suicidal thoughts during their school years.

Vestibular stimulation and happiness.

When I started to collect research data on children and vestibular stimulation exercises, I discovered that children who were put through these specific activities became much happier and we didn't understand why. We were trying to help them with their particular learning issues, so we were surprised when we also saw their emotional strength improve substantially.

I went back to the psychologists and neuroscientists to get them to explain exactly what was going on. In the last few years, we have discovered the very part of the brain that we stimulate to increase skill development is the same part of the brain that's responsible for improving mental robustness, and with that, emotional control. Wow! It was another accidental discovery, that I wish I could take the credit, but I can't.

Balance, mood, emotions.

Digging into research is fun, especially when we realised that lives were being changed for the better. Research shows us that lots of balance stimulation in childhood is crucial to the development of our emotional controls. It explains why some people are emotionally sensitive and it gives a huge clue about a possible solution if they aren't. Some of this research goes back to the 1930's and, 80 years on hardly anyone has heard about it. How many lives would have been so different had this been pieced together earlier?

We started using vestibular (balance) exercises to build up essential skills, make life easier and at the same time free up some mental capacity, in other words, give us more "thinking capacity". When we saw children also get happier, our initial theory was that the extra mental capacity we helped create made them feel calmer, and that was true but now we realised was only part of the story.

Childhood memories in the brain.

What's become increasingly clear is that those same exercises we have created also strengthen the very connections in the brain that controls our emotions.

Hang on in here with me for a few minutes, it's getting a bit technical, but it is so interesting. When we have any experience that makes us "feel" any emotion, whether good or bad, the brain stores that as a memory. It stores the event together with the emotion that you experienced. The "librarian" in the brain that stores these emotional memories is called the amygdala.

So, if something scares you badly as a child, it is stored as a subconscious event with a strong link to extreme fear. The amygdala also stores good memories too, but bad memories where you felt pain or fear are much more powerful memories and will have far greater influence on thoughts and decisions in the future. When you are making any decisions, the amygdala will throw these emotional memories on one side or the other of the scales of the "shall I/shan't I" consideration. For instance, if you enjoy the experience of eating sugar, every time you get the chance to have more, the amygdala will be subconsciously saying "do it, do it", and the chances are that you will. However the amygdala doesn't use actual words that we hear in our thoughts when it's putting pressure on us to do something, or not do it, it uses strong influence but doesn't say "why" in words, we just "feel it" in our sub-conscious.

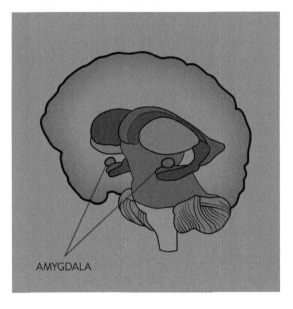

AMYGDALA

Amygdala - protects us from harm.

In prehistoric times when life was much more dangerous, and we were surrounded by life-threatening dangers, our brains developed a way of helping our genes survive. The amygdala stored memories of things that had hurt or scared us so that when another serious threat appeared we'd go straight into a "fight, flight or freeze" state. The control of your whole body, movement and actions are constantly handed over to a very primitive part of the brain, and you have no more choices for a while - you are in "fight, flight or freeze" mode. At the same time, the brain also releases chemicals so you are ready for every eventuality. No doubt it has saved many lives and kept our species alive and well.

Struggling children feel threatened.

So why is this relevant to your child? When the emotional response wiring is not well developed, the "threat" sensor gets too sensitive, and your child will have far too many false alarms.

This is hyper-sensitivity and can cause panic attacks. For emotional stability, the amygdala (the librarian keeping track of these feelings and risks) must be connected to our logical brain, so we don't make bad, quick decisions and get over emotional - but in the fight or flight state all connections to our "logic" are broken so we just focus on survival.

When the balance mechanism hasn't been fully stimulated the wiring needed in the brain is not fully completed. We have weak, inadequate controls of our feelings and emotions. The brain tries hard to make sense of everything that is happening to us at any time. But it gets confused if we haven't automatized (learnt) how to deal with any given new situation. So, without warning, without checking whether this is a real threat or an imaginary threat, we are put straight into fight or flight mode. When in that state, there is no point saying "pull yourself together" because all mental links to anything logical in your brain are cut for the moment and you just have to ride out this storm until calmness returns.

People that struggle with poor emotional control don't choose to be that way; they don't enjoy it. In fact, they often feel like they are going to die. The sense of threat really is that great, even though the reality is that there is no threat to worry about. A lot of understanding and sympathy is called for.

Solution - vestibular stimulation.

The bonus of developing the vestibular connections is it can lead to mental strength, emotional robustness and the peace that comes from having a logical mind. In that state you are able to put things into perspective and make calmer decisions. This is what we eventually learnt working with so many children. At last, we were able to understand why their anxiety and panic attacks became less frequent. One of my sons suffered from severe anxiety for some time, and I was amazed and perplexed by the ignorance and dreadful advice he was given by some of his medical advisors.

Today he is free of these challenges and vestibular training was an important part of his healing process.

Recap.

So, in this chapter, I have shown you why so many of the symptoms that we THINK are psychological/psychiatric might have been misread. I have told you about the misunderstandings that exist within our modern education system. I have shown you that there is hope for your child if their symptoms are cerebellum related. The plasticity of the brain is remarkable; it means that your brain can be made ready to learn at any age. Before we get started on how to test if this is relevant for your child, let me give you some of the secrets and science behind this amazing opportunity to create more grey matter in a brain.

◆ ◆ ◆

Jed's Story

Jed was a troubled little child who lacked confidence. At school teachers would say Jed was a cry baby who'd well up with tears easily and often be lost looking out of the window. He never wanted to take part joining in with other school friends when they played football on the playground. When we started Zing, after the 3 months the school contacted us to say there had been an enormous improvement in Jed, he'd started playing with the other children. The biggest improvements we saw were at the 6 month mark as he joined a karate and surf club. School called us in to talk about the national tests he'd done and were happy to report that he had come in at the 99th percentile!! I would recommend it to any parent as it's such a small amount of time to devote but so worthwhile as it releases their potential and I also felt that Jed felt the benefits too.

(Claire Purdy, Mother)

CHAPTER 4

THE TRUTH THAT HAS BEEN HIDDEN FROM YOU

"What makes a child gifted and talented may not always be good grades in school, but a different way of looking at the world and learning."
Chuck Grassley

veryone else may have given up on your child for various reasons, but what if most of the problems your child is facing are happening because of misunderstandings? How would that make you feel? I will tell you how it made ME feel. It made me feel very determined. It made me want to change the whole system. That is why I have written this book.

My heart is with parents who are not supported in their longing to see their children happy, learning and succeeding. I was one of those parents. I spent too many sleepless nights worrying about my own daughter, who couldn't read, write, make friends or learn. I have spent too many hours in school meetings where nobody understood what she was going through. I know exactly what it is like to be a worried parent who just does not accept being told that there is nothing we can do, especially when it is not true.

The secret about your struggling child.

I was shocked (and still am) over the amount of research out there that can help our children, research that no one has pieced together until now. It baffles me that this is not common knowledge because it explains why your child is struggling and why your child is often misunderstood, it even offers a solution.

In this chapter, I will:

1. Explain why the establishment is largely ignoring this research.
2. Explain the hidden root cause of the most common learning and behavioural issues.
3. The surprising way to help your child turn back time and recover the learning that you thought they'd missed with simple brain/body co-ordination exercises that seem to press the "reset button" on their learning ability.

Why the hidden root cause has been kept from you.

I really do not want to think that anyone intentionally holds back this research from you, but what surprised me as a dad, is that such a lot of exciting research gets buried, sometimes for generations. There might be two reasons for this;

Firstly:

Research only sees the light of day if some organisation has a commercial interest to bring that research to you. In other words, if they are going to make money out of it! So this research I'm sharing with you is unlikely to make anybody rich, (I have personally spent nearly 20 years and many millions of pounds to research and test this) As a disruptive entrepreneur/researcher/warrior/dad, I see its importance because I have seen it transform countless lives and I hope your child will become another of them.

Secondly:

When seasoned academics have been thoroughly investigating a specific line of research for many years they tend to stay wedded to their ideas. So they're reluctant to endorse new, breakthrough ideas that make their research obsolete because it hurts them, and their reputations are in jeopardy. What am I sharing with you are breakthroughs from major universities around the world.

From my perspective, it is now possible to change the lives of children with learning and behavioural/mood issues. We no longer need to regard most learning and behavioural issues as lifetime sentences or unsolvable problems. We now have the tools and knowledge to understand them. We must now look at this from a neurological perspective rather than focusing only on the psychological.

Why you need to access and stimulate your child's brain.

What became clear to the researchers in my clinic, was that we had to find a way to test each child's brain individually and then invent exercises that could mimic the stimulation that allowed the brain to finish its job of developing the specific skills that each child had missed out on.

This may surprise you, but researchers proved to me that it is possible to reset the way the brain works, not by doing brain training which is so popular today but by stimulating the cerebellum, an area of the brain at the back of your head. When you stimulate it in the right way, (and that varies from person to person), it can even go back in time to find incompletely developed brain skills just waiting to be finished off!

What we've discovered from research is that it's now possible to help your child by stimulating the cerebellum and pressing the "reset" button and they complete the development of skills your child has struggled with until now. This brain/body connection is so amazing it is called the "brain within the brain" and by forcing a reset, you can continue the development of the brain in a completely natural and a highly effective way. I've seen it transform countless children.

The (misunderstood) brain within your child's brain.

The brain/body connection, the cerebellum, was overlooked for decades by most neuroscientists. Even when they took pictures of the brain, some didn't bother to include it in their photographs, they completely missed the importance of it, and a few still do. They assumed it was just there for balance and co-ordination of the body, and of course it does fulfil that role.

In the 1990's, a researcher from Harvard University discovered that the cerebellum was doing far, far more than that. Eventually, he started calling it, "the brain within the brain" because it has such an important role. Think of it as the part of the brain that "matures" us and hardwires the rest of brain to create skills and automate processes to make our life easy.

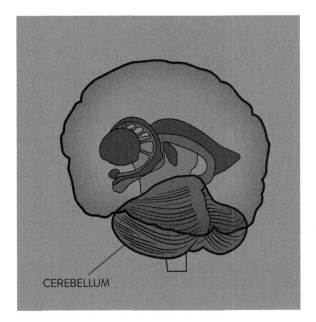

CEREBELLUM

In your child's case, it determines whether your child will be able to read easily or not, write or not, behave well or not, play a sport well or not, develop good social skills or not, and so on.

Why is your child's brain underdeveloped?

Why is the cerebellum not developing the way it should? We really don't know the complete answer to that question. Actually I am not that interested in "why", but I am passionate about how to support the brain to finish its role in developing key skills. I am obsessed with finding out how best to help the cerebellum and stimulate development, so those skills become more effortless, automatic and natural. This is <u>what</u> I have spent the last 20 years doing. Finding out what caused the problem in the first place may well take another 20 years or more. Families need solutions, and they need them now.

How can we change the brain?

How can we even change the brain and finish the development? This is a bit like "insider information" as so few know about it, so I am excited to share it with you. The cerebellum is driven by stimulation of our inner ear, our balance organ (or vestibular). When our balance organ is working properly, the cerebellum is stimulated to do what it is supposed to do. It is the electrician in the brain wiring up all of the processes and skills we need so we can learn, have skills, control emotions, make good decisions, be resourceful and achieve. Ultimately to have an easy life.

I watched a lamb being born in the spring, and within seconds it was standing up and starting to feed. The next day it was running around the field. The cerebellum of a sheep is highly developed at birth so it can balance, stand, walk and run. The cerebellum in humans develops much more slowly and takes 2-3 years to get to where most animals are when they're born. This relatively slow maturing process in human brains often fails to be completed. The consequences of that can show up when a child goes to school.

Your child's challenges in a modern world.

The slow, steady development of the cerebellum happens in the early months and years of a child's life, when it's crawling, tumbling, wobbling and pulling itself up on the furniture to start taking its first tentative steps. The crazy things a baby does stimulates the vestibular (the balance organ) and develops the capabilities of the cerebellum. The brain actually NEEDS challenges to develop. When this happens, the cerebellum becomes better at wiring up the rest of the brain, rather like a super talented electrician wiring up connections to create all the important brain/body processes and skills.

Life for a human child has changed through the centuries, and some aspects are no longer natural. Baby walkers, TV's, smartphones and tablets, even our passive lifestyles affect development. The development of the cerebellum is critical to a child becoming a fully functioning human being that has no struggles. Have we moved too far away from nature and the natural environment and lifestyle that were designed to fully develop our brains neurologically? Are children now paying the price?

Don't encourage a baby to walk too soon.

Encouraging a baby to walk before they can crawl is an example of how we can unwittingly interfere with and hamper development in the brain. Crawling plays a vital part in your child's brain developed. Therefore, as parents we should actively encourage this phase even if your child could miss it and go straight to walking.

What I have worked on for nearly 20 years is understanding how we can stimulate the vestibular system and thereby drive the development of the cerebellum at any age, to go back in time and redo the job, and this time finish it. A "reset" button for the brain. It sounds reasonably easy, but we soon realised that every human brain is very different. Every brain develops differently, which explains why we have huge variations in our character, our skills and our abilities.

How your child becomes a natural at things.

I want to explain how the brain/body connection develops so that your child creates the skills they need.

When we learnt to ride a bike, we knew in our mind what we had to do as we had watched others do it, but when we tried ourselves, we fell off, got hurt and bruised our knees.

We tried again, and we fell off again, and that happened time and time again. After hours of practice, we started to ride, wobbled a bit at first, but there came the point where it seemed as if suddenly it was all easy, automatic and effortless, and we didn't have to think about it at all after that.

What was going on in the brain? We went from "trying and falling off" to "riding without thinking". This process to make riding automatic was being worked out by the cerebellum - and it's a typical "learning" process. While you were dangling about, falling off and bruising yourself, the brain was busy wiring up the circuits (learning) so that balance, pedalling, steering and braking became totally automatic. Eventually you can ride without having to "think" about what you were doing at all. The truth is that when we have to "think" about what we do, the brain processing speed is very slow and not precise enough so that things go wrong, so whilst learning to ride we fall off.

Learning to ride a bike - and everything else in life.

You need to practise, stretch the brain and hardwire every skill in life. Reading, listening, moving our eyes, social skills, running, dancing, sports, writing, talking, loving, EVERYTHING. The cerebellum needs to create the "automatic wiring", rather like a computer programmer creates a programme so that every process becomes consistent, automatic, and effortless. When we're "thinking hard" about riding a bike, we're falling off because we're doing our processing in our thinking brain. And, in many children, some important skills never gets fully developed and hardwired. This means that they have to "think about them", so they struggle, often get into overload and lose emotional control and focus.

Why you don't want your child to use the slow "thinking brain" for key skills.

It is no surprise that a child with an incompletely developed cerebellum struggles as they have to use the thinking brain far more than they should. The thinking brain is SLOW, terribly slow when compared to a fully automatized skill? Many neuroscientists argue it may be a MILLION times slower when we have to still "think" about how to use a skill. That's why we want all of our day-to-day skills processed automatically without using any "thinking" capacity. This will save us from being wrongly accused of being slow, lazy or stupid.

I put my bike in the garden shed when I was about 18 as I'd just discovered how much fun cars were, and didn't use again until I was in my late 30s. So, for about 20 years, I wasn't practising riding a bike at all but, when I pulled my bike out of the garden shed, pumped up the tyres and jumped on it, I'd still got the brain circuitry to enable me to ride automatically. It was still there. It was still working perfectly, and I rode my bike without having to think about it. That's how good the cerebellum is at wiring up skills we need and those skills last long-term.

The cerebellum, the brain/body connection, has to be developed so that these skills are created properly. You can have a perfect brain and a perfect body, but if the brain/body connection isn't working properly, all sorts of things will go wrong. If its social skills that your child struggles with, it will be one or more areas in the cerebellum that aren't fully developed so the wiring of those skills won't be complete. If it's reading, it will be another set of skills unfinished. If it's concentration, it'll be another set of skills - and so on. It always comes back to the development of the relevant parts of our brain: body connection and the development of appropriate skills and processes needed to make them effortless, consistent and natural.

Finding the undiscovered potential in the brain.

I have shared my observation that most struggling children have MORE, not LESS, potential than their friends in school, but it gets even better. You have probably heard that you only use a tiny part of your brain, but no one has told you how you can use the rest of it. That is what I am about to tell you. The great news is that cerebellum is the clue. To develop the cerebellum starts with stimulation of the inner ear, the balance organ, in a way that excites the cerebellum and readies it to learn. You may have read about plasticity in the brain; this is the readiness of the brain to acquire new skills and processes. We used to think that the brain is only "plastic" when we are young, but, we now know that plasticity remains throughout the whole of our lives, and that's exciting news for all of us.

Why every child need different exercises.

It would be great if we could give a single set of exercises that every family member could do and the cerebellum would reach its full potential. Sadly, everybody's brain is unique because it has been wired up differently, and the process of giving the right stimulation to the right area of the brain is just too complex, so the best solution also needs to be customised to suit that brain. Later, I will tell you how to get started to find the exercises that your child's brain could benefit from.

My team of researchers have studied many different ways to assess the development of the brain/body connection and establish precisely the level and type of the stimulation. Different types of stimulation of the inner ear are achieved by doing different balance and movement exercises.

No brain is quite like your child's.

To mature the cerebellum effectively, every child needs a completely individualised programme. This was a big "A-ha!" moment for both myself and the doctors and neuroscientists I worked with. A one-size-fits-all approach will provide some benefit but is unlikely to find all of the hidden potential.

We had to do countless experiments to find stimulation and coordination exercises that mimic the development in the cerebellum in the way that it should have happened in the first place. We learned how to test each child so that we could carefully select the appropriate stimulations that naturally continue and complete the process. It's not an instant process, not like taking a pill, but it is comforting to know that it is replicating a completely natural process, one that has a lasting impact too. When this is done correctly, you create more brain cells in the cerebellum and increase the density of grey matter there. So to summarise, your child's brain needs a systematised process, customised with specific exercises, targeting the vestibular - that in turn stimulates the cerebellum - that in turn creates the skills that, up to now, had been missing.

The secret of a super learner's brain.

When skills are fully developed, they are stored in the brain in its long-term memory, where the capacity is almost infinite. The speed of brain processing is almost infinite too, blisteringly fast. When everyday "actions" or "skills" are hard-wired properly, you don't have to "think" when you do them. You just "do them" naturally, effortlessly, instantly. However, all of the skills that are still underdeveloped require "thinking about" in the thinking brain where the processing is much, much slower, much harder work mentally and to cap it all the skill is not performed so precisely either.

So, if the cerebellum hasn't created the complete set of important skills that you need to perform everyday tasks, then you will need to process things in your thinking brain. It's a busy place, and the chances are high that it's going to go into overload. When we feel stressed, it is because our thinking brain is overloaded. When we are forgetful, or we have a poor short-term memory, it's when our thinking brain is overloaded. When we make poor or "short-term" decisions instead of making a more considered decision, it's because our thinking brain is overloaded.

When we lose emotional control of focus, it's the same thing.

The impact of having underdeveloped skills places a huge the burden on our thinking brain. The space in our thinking brain is precious, rather like the RAM in our computer. Most people can only cope with about seven different things in their thinking brain, and that's not a lot, so when it's full, it's full. When it's full, we forget things. When it's full, life is not easy.

Incredible hope – the brain stores what your child has tried to learn.

Here is the most incredible breakthrough on my journey to find a solution for my daughter. In the beginning, she was one of our first "guinea pigs". We tested her performance every month, and every day she did balance, and other stimulatory exercises customised to her brain's needs. One day, something remarkable happened. She suddenly started to read at the age of 27. Up to this time, we believed that she had not learnt ANYTHING about reading, she could not read a sentence. Suddenly she was reading magazines. I was in shock, so were our doctors.

This was a very emotional experience for me. Tears were in my eyes as I watched and listened to her read. I watched her quickly develop the ability to concentrate. I saw her ability to join social discussions in a way she'd never have had the confidence to do before. The changes were remarkable. Had we given her any of those skills? No, impossible, that's not what we were doing. The teaching and learning had gone on many years earlier - but the wiring of the skills had not been finished off. The exercises that she'd done were rather like an electrician who's spent many months wiring up a building, and then, when the job is finished he simply puts the fuse in and "the lights come on". What we had achieved was to make the final connections and revealed her hidden potential.

My biggest break-through.

I had so many butterflies and excitement that I could not sleep properly for weeks, this was a MAJOR breakthrough. It seemed that the brain had stored the attempts my daughter had made to learn, waiting for the cerebellum to develop so it could finish the job and she could use them. Was this a one-off? Would others have the same effect? A few weeks went by, and sure enough, more children (and adults) had exactly the same experience.

An extreme and encouraging case was of an 82-year-old woman who had never been able to read or write. She begged me to let her do the exercise programme. Incredibly, after four months she was on national television telling her story, showing the first letter she had written in her life. This was incredible.

Wonderful cases just kept knocking on our door.

Teenager: From OCD and anxiety to happiness.

Andre was a lad that had many challenging symptoms. He had obsessive-compulsive behaviour with a lot of rituals; he did a lot of stemming. Life was extremely hard for the family because he had to go through these ritualistic processes constantly, or he could not cope. Unless he was allowed to do them, he became completely unbalanced and anxious. The family could never take him into new situations, and at school he struggled badly with learning and with making social connections with others of his age. In the act of desperation, his mom put him on our vestibular stimulation programme to see if it could support and develop his cerebellum. The changes in Andre were enormous, and within weeks his behaviour was changing significantly. The things they thought he was unable to do normally, he started doing. The behaviour they had found impossible to correct seemed to naturally correct itself. Within months he'd become a calm, rational, happy young lad. Had we taught him those skills?

Adults can benefit too.

Later I was introduced to a woman in her 40's that had never read a book. She is delightful, bright, has a responsible job (that doesn't involve reading of course), but really low self-esteem. She was always sensitive to the fact that she couldn't do some critical things that other people find easy. Her passion was animals, and she longed to read about and pursue her study of animals. I told her that if she exercised her cerebellum, she'd read a book within a few months. She thought I was exaggerating, but she was desperate to overcome this tragic limitation, so she agreed to do it.

I pointed out to her that it meant that she'd have to do some online brain tests and do some special physical exercises for 10 minutes, twice a day for the next few months. She asked, "Is that all?" and then agreed to do it. Four months to the day later, I had the thrill of getting a picture sent from her phone showing three thick books that she had already read. Imagine how her self-esteem was rising. From then her life has taken an amazing upturn, she is now a far more confident woman transformed in all areas of her life. She can do the things that she couldn't before, those things that others find simple; she can now do, it's thrilling to see her progress.

I long for the day that every child that's struggling gets this chance because it will have become standard practice in every school. Who knows when that will be the reality? Until then it is down to parents to give their child this opportunity.

"Catch-up" time for children who haven't learned in school.

This is something that all teachers need to know. When they are teaching children who seem to be unable to learn, far more than they realise is being retained. The child just can't find or use that skill or knowledge, yet!

No, they have partly developed already within his cerebellum, but couldn't be used until the final piece of wiring had been put into place.

So a message to teachers; "Don't feel disheartened - keep doing the right thing even though you can't yet see the progress, your teaching is achieving more than you think".

Don't be jealous of children who thrive in school. If you've got a child that appears to have missed out on learning at school, then this is great news for you too. More has probably been stored than you realise, it's just not yet completed the final phase of its development, but, it is still waiting there to be finished off.

I also own a private school which focusses on creating a world-class environment and learning practices for children. I am a huge fan of good teachers and their ability to inspire, and I make it my job to study education. It baffles me that there is so much misunderstanding about what schools achieve. Parents assume that if their child is top of the class, then they are going to do wonderful things in life, they are all set. However, research doesn't show that at all. Research done at Boston University followed the highest achievers (Valedictorians) from a number of schools. It showed that the highest achievers went on to have successful careers, often in the top tier jobs. However, they don't become famous entrepreneurs or leaders in their fields. The surprise was that the innovators, entrepreneurs and creatives had come from way down in the pecking order of the school class.

The good news is that if your child isn't currently achieving, then there is a process likely to find any hidden potential and give the child the chance you'd love them to have.

This is NOT anything like brain-training.

So, the cerebellum can be developed by stimulation through carefully chosen physical exercises. And to achieve that these exercises must involve balance and coordination. When we do carefully chosen activities, our friend, the cerebellum, becomes excited and primed, ready to develop new skills in the brain. It's time to learn. Just to be quite clear, this is entirely different to brain training. So many had great hope in brain-training, and doubtless, it can improve already existing skills, but it seems not effective in the creation of completely new skills, and generally, it's the new skills that our children need.

This is why labels are not the way to go.

I've had the thrill of working with tens of thousands of children and observe what happens when you support and focus on the cerebellum. I have seen parents and teachers totally surprised about the level of intellect that was hidden, waiting to be discovered, in those children that everyone had given up on.

One of the problems with our education system is that there is so much pressure to put a label on a child if they are struggling. Labels always focus on external symptoms. They never focus on the potential that the child may have, and they never address what we now know is the root cause of these issues. So, my attitude to labels has changed significantly since I started unearthing research around this subject.

Labels are a permanent mark, rather like a tattoo. It has a huge impact on a child and everyone around them, right into adulthood. A label doesn't ever go away. Labels reduce expectations, when, in fact, it should be increasing expectations. It is so cruel to give a child a permanent label when there is a chance that the symptoms that they're suffering from can be rectified. My strong belief is that far greater care needs to be given before any label is applied.

Many of the highest achievers drop out of school or college.

If you study the education of famous billionaires, entrepreneurs, researchers and other leaders, you will find many dropped out of school or college. How can that be? Our education system is geared up to look after the 80% of children in the middle of the stream, the ones that fit the normal expectations. The system is not geared up to find hidden genius, hence they are the ones that are misunderstood. They don't fit in or belong so, understandably, they drop out. How tragic is that? How many genii spend the whole of their lives undiscovered?

If children are struggling or frustrated in any way, then the cause of their issues must be investigated. With some, it is obvious that they are bright in many aspects but aren't learning in the usual way. They drop out of school because their reading isn't strong or their behaviour isn't brilliant, or sometimes it is because they're under stimulated. These are issues that mean they won't easily fit into the "middle of the road" production line of the school system. There are many humorous examples of very high achievers who had been told by a teacher when they left school that they're "not going to make much of their life". That may seem funny now but believe me, it wouldn't have been funny at the time. But how could they get it that wrong? How could they miss the hidden genius?

The brain has infinite capacity.

The practice of writing off and labelling children because they're struggling must stop. If instead of the label said "Huge hidden potential" it would probably be more appropriate. Many assumptions about the limitations of the brain are wrong because if we go about it the right way, its potential is almost limitless. Research that can lead to such transformation of lives is out there.

Why has this been hidden from you?

I am puzzled why every teacher training curriculum doesn't include detailed neurological explanations for the process of learning and the cause of common learning issues. Good teachers long to find solutions for the children that struggle. They want every child to learn what they're teaching. Yet, in a class of 30, there will often be five children who don't take it in. Schools must change. The foundation of learning is neurological, and there is little point in starting to teach a child unless that neurological foundation is solid.

I've made it my job to bring the research about "learning" to parents and teachers. Research that could have changed lives has remained buried for decades in some cases. Your child needs the benefits of it now and can't afford to wait.

So this is a book of hope, with details of research-based practical things that you can do to get your child to where he or she deserves to be so that they don't suffer and struggle needlessly.

When will this reach everyone?

We need to get this to as many children as possible as quickly as we can.

Every time I see my daughter I feel so grateful that she survived her depression. She has been my inspiration to continue the research and to ensure it reaches as many as possible. Of course, I wish I could have reached her when she was still at school, but that didn't happen. If you recognise in your child some of the symptoms described in this book my heart goes out to you, and I wish you well in your quest to help them display you've not seen, YET!

♦ ♦ ♦

Andre's Story

Andre was struggling with Autism, OCD and some sleep nightmares. He couldn't fall asleep, lying awake until 1am or 2am, making him very tired the next day. At the worst he couldn't go to school and would sit at home banging his head against the wall not wanting to live anymore. Andre is now a lot calmer and we have fun together, there is a lot of happiness in the house. He's getting on much better at school and his results have improved. For the first time, and this feels horrible to say but for the first time in his life I see the shine in his eyes.

(Violah Vandfoss, Mother)

CHAPTER 5

TEST YOUR CHILD'S SYMPTOMS
- THE MORE THERE IS, THE
MORE POTENTIAL FOR CHANGE

"The true sign of intelligence is not knowledge but imagination."
Albert Einstein

Struggling kids are misunderstood and mistreated because of 'bad' signs that might actively be good signs.

Here is the old school way of looking at your child's symptoms: The more problems, the worse it is.

Here is the new way of looking at your child's symptoms from a brain perspective: The more symptoms the more undiscovered potential, and hope.

So do go through the following symptoms summary and tick those that you recognise in your child. The more symptoms you tick, the higher the likelihood of a link to the cerebellum. Later in the book, I am going to share with you how to get started on the reset process, redeveloping the cerebellum.

Symptom tracker and new hope.

These are a number of seemingly unconnected symptoms that could point to the cause being the development of the cerebellum?

You probably place significant focus on the most concerning symptom in your child. For some, it's concentration. For some, it's reading. For some it's behaviour. For some, it's poor social skills. But often the most obvious or concerning symptom is the tip of the iceberg. In my daughter's case, I focused on her reading skills even though there were much other "lesser" issues. It shocked me when I studied large numbers of children that there is a long list of symptoms and all are linked to the cerebellum. Nobody had told me about the common root cause.

Surprising symptom checklist.

But don't expect your child to have all of the symptoms, just make a note of which symptoms do apply to your child.

Slow reading, poor comprehension.

The surprise for many parents of children who take F-O-R-E-V-E-R to read even a sentence in a book is that it is poor eye movement skills almost always cause poor reading and not low intelligence. You could well find that the child has a more powerful brain than those good readers in the class. One in four children struggle with reading; they face the embarrassment of not being able to do what others find easy AND they are so misunderstood. It's often assumed that they're not trying hard enough or, even worse, it's assumed that they must be unintelligent. You're likely to worry a lot about your child's reading skills as I did about my own daughter. Life, both at school and after school, is incredibly difficult when you cannot read.

Eye movement (or eye-tracking) is the ability to track words and letters smoothly as we read them, so they go into our brain in the right order. When your child's visual tracking isn't perfect, reading becomes a nightmare, and for many impossible. Scarily, the standard treatment for dealing with poor reading is to focus on the problem, in other words, give them more reading practice. It's also been fashionable in recent years to teach them "phonics". This may help some a little but it won't surprise you that this does not correct the root cause of the problem.

The child needs effective eye tracking, and to achieve this will need a combination of vestibular and eye tracking exercises.

These should be selected based on the child's individual needs to finish the development of their eye tracking skills, and when that is complete, you could well find that the child's reading improves significantly. They had the "reading skills" all the time, but the brain wasn't seeing the letters in the right order to make sense of them.

How to test whether eye tracking is making your child struggle.

If poor reading is something that affects your child, then do try this simple test - it may be enough to demonstrate the reason behind their issue. Get your child to hold their head very still. Hold your index finger about one foot (30 cm) in front of the eyes and move it slowly back and forth from side to side. Get them to track your index finger with his eyes. Keep checking the head; children tend to move their head rather than the eyes themselves. Sometimes children's eye tracking is so poor that you can see little jumps in their eyes instead of it being a smooth movement. If you can see any unevenness or jumps, then this is confirmation that they have poor eye tracking.

This has significant implications for how easy, or not, reading is for them.

Sometimes the jumping is not significant enough to be visible to the naked eye but is still poor enough to cause reading issues - many opticians have the equipment to show this if you want to be certain.

Poor handwriting.

When words and letters look like an uneven wave of chaos on the paper - teachers and parents can get really worried. Don´t. Don't call the child lazy, clumsy, sloppy, unfocused or unintelligent either. The reason is usually NOT lack of talent or brains. It may even be the opposite. When I see it; I expect to find big brains and a lack of what is called fine motor controls. Many of these children have great ideas in their head, but struggle to get them down in writing. Their mind is in complete overload when they try and write, and it causes them a lot of frustration. Writing skills are closely linked to eye-tracking skills. The same part of the brain that controls your pen also controls how you move your eyes. It is called a "fine motor skill" and if there is a problem in one area then there nearly always is in the other.

Thus most children that don't enjoy reading don't find writing easy either. If your child is a reluctant writer, only writes small amounts and probably in a rather scruffy way too – they are not choosing to write badly - it is probably an incompletely developed fine motor skill.

Holding their pen in a strange way.

Does your child hold a pen in a funny way when writing? If so, check if they use (move) the whole of their fingers (or even the whole hand) to write? This is also a sign of underdeveloped fine motor skills. We are supposed to write with (and only move) the tips of the fingers. If your child uses the whole of the fingers or hand, it is a great sign of scope for further development in the cerebellum. It is usually a waste of time to force this child to practise writing when it is cerebellum-stimulation exercises that are needed. In this case, practice rarely helps much. This child is using another part of the brain (and hence another part of their fingers) to write. So for them, holding the pen in an untypical way is a compensatory strategy, as the usual method for holding and controlling the pen to write is not an option.

I've seen many instances, where children that are poor at handwriting are good at drawing and art. That's because drawing is a different skill controlled by a different part of the brain, the part that uses gross motor movements. So it is logical that some may have good skills in art but struggle when it comes to handwriting. A few such children are often capable of holding their pen strangely and achieving neat writing - they are actually drawing the letters - usually quite slowly but, nevertheless, readable.

Poor spelling.

For children that have poor eye tracking (see above), spelling is a very difficult task. The eyes jump around and often the letters that they see do too. When I talk to a family about spelling and reading problems I will often ask the child "Do the letters move and jump around when you try to read?". Generally the child replies "yes", and it often takes the parents by surprise. Mom then asks; "why have you never told us?" to which the child replies, "I thought the letters jump around for everybody". To this day most schools never check for this easily detected problem, isn't that baffling?

It's pointless trying to teach them how to spell a word when they almost certainly will have forgotten it the next day. Every time they look at that word their poor eye-tracking skill means that they "see" the letters in a different order, it's a nightmare.

What does make a difference is eye -tracking and cerebellum-stimulation exercises that focus on the part of the brain where the problem lies.

Poor concentration.

When a child can't concentrate, it is a nightmare for the child, the parents and the teachers. When a child is restless, unable to sit still, gazing out of the window or fiddling instead of listening then frustration and tension sets in. Most assume that a child who can't focus and listen is not making an effort. This is not the case. Typically this child is trying very hard to maintain focus, and they aren't choosing to have poor concentration.

It's probably impossible for them to focus on one thing for long, the attention area of the brain is overloaded, sometimes caused by the incomplete development of their listening (auditory processing) skills. But parent meetings can lead to concentration and attention issues turning into a medical condition with a label before the root cause is determined. The good news is that there are effective physical exercise solutions that stimulate the very part of the brain that could enable your child to focus and concentrate far more easily.

Not crawling much as a baby.

Many of the children that struggle at school didn't crawl for the normal amount of time. Many parents are proud of the fact that their child is walking around the furniture at nine months, "Aren't they advanced?" they say, but that optimism is misguided. They may be bypassing some critical elements of development and setting the child up for struggles later. If I see a mom encouraging her child to walk around the furniture too soon, I cringe. Let them crawl from 9 months or so for about three or four months before they walk. Don't encourage them to shuffle on their bottom either, that also doesn't seem to be a good idea, crawling correctly for three or four months seems the best option.

A few children crawl for a much longer time than that. They'll start crawling a little later, and they crawl for maybe six months or more and start walking at 15 to 18 months. These are all clues that development isn't happening in quite the right order and quite the right way that it ought to and the cerebellum will probably not develop in the way it should. In my experience at least one in three children who struggle bypassed part of the crawling phase of development.

That is why I don't recommend devices that hold a baby so they use only their legs, rather than crawling on all 4's - I believe that they are potentially dangerous.

My eldest daughter was the only one of my four children to use such a device, and it might well have contributed to her later struggles. It's not a risk I'd take again.

Pregnancy and birth trauma.

Quite a proportion of children that struggle when they get to school had some trauma in pregnancy and/or birth. Now, I don't want mothers to start thinking, "it's all my fault", that's not the case. You have to look at what's the root cause and what's the effect. I suspect that difficulties during pregnancy or birth are more likely to be the "effect" rather than the "cause".

Ear problems - infections, grommets and perforated eardrums.

From early on in my research, I was amazed by the number of struggling children who have had ear infections or grommets fitted, some even had suffered perforated eardrums. It's bad enough for them having to cope with the pain, but the implications for the future could be significant too. Many of these "ear-problem children" show signs of learning or developmental issue as they progress through school. Why?

The inner ear, the balance mechanisms and the auditory processing mechanisms all are heavily involved in the development of learning, emotional and other brain processes. The sensations or feelings generated here are so important for the development of mental capacity. The correct sensory information must be transmitted from the inner ear; this is hampered when your child suffers from these issues in developing years.

If this has contributed to the problems then a good solution is vestibular stimulating exercises, these continue and help complete what was not finalised when they were younger. More on this later.

Messiness.

Clothes on the floor. Food left on the dining table. Chaos in the room. Gym clothes, lost socks and lunch boxes scattered all over the county. Yep, some children are far, far messier than others. Your child seems blissfully unaware, except for during your occasional meltdowns. It IS infuriating, right? Why is this happening?

The answer is quite surprising, and no, your child may not be deliberately lazy! The reason why a child doesn't "think" about being tidy is that they don't have the spare mental capacity to think about it. There is not enough RAM to consider "where should I put this, so it is neat and tidy?". When you have plenty of mental capacity that process becomes automatic, in your subconscious. Messy children have an overload in the working memory part of their brain. Unless there's capacity to be organised in their brain they haven't got a chance to being organised in their life. And when you're not organised in your brain, neither is your bedroom. Neither is your desk. You're going to be forgetful. You're going to be disorganised, and your child is likely to be blamed for behaviour that they have no mental capacity to change.

The good news is that you can increase the free space in working memory and reclaim the lost socks and the lack of structure in your life. More on this later.

Clumsiness and (lack of) sporting skills.

Approximately one in eight children are clumsy. Don't assume that they're choosing to be that way or that they could change it if they really wanted to. This is far from the truth, and I cringe when parents tell a child to "be more careful" - they often don't have the mental capacity to be careful even though they'd love to be. Clumsiness is yet another of those misunderstood conditions that make children feel wrong and ashamed. Not only do they knock things over and bang into people, but they're also less likely to be called to play in a team sport. They don't have the co-ordination to catch and kick balls accurately. Some who are only partially affected by this enjoy some individual sports, but it's rare that they get to participate in a team sport. This is something they can't change quickly unless you help them stimulate the appropriate part of their brain.

Poor balance.

The effect of incompletely developed balance and coordination is very common, but you may not notice it at first. It often indirectly impacts your child's ability to fully develop some basic skills, including things like reading and concentration. It can have a significant effect on the development of emotional control too. There are three main contributors to our ability to balance:

1. The feelings we get through our body.
2. The sensory input from our balance organ (the inner ear).
3. The information we take in through our eyes.

All of these inputs must be automatically coordinated in our brain for us to have perfect balance, but for some - they just aren't. Good balance is quite misunderstood. When I speak about this, most parents of struggling children say, "Oh, my child's balance is great". So, I ask them to make them stand on one leg with their eyes closed and see what happens. I warn them, of course, "Be careful because you may be very surprised about how quickly your child falls over" and that often proves to be the case. A sure sign of poor balance. So this is a fascinating topic, balance and coordination skills in children are often capable of much further development, with surprising consequences to many aspects of your child's life.

Some children that have very little balance input to their brain from the vestibular become good skiers, skaters or windsurfers. Why?

Because the poor input from the vestibular forces the brain to develop a greater reliance on feelings through the body and so they "feel" their balance through their legs to a far greater content than average.

So, can your child stand on one leg with the eyes closed for very long? If not, there is more development to complete and with it comes the probability that they'll find it easier to learn new skills.

Short-term and long-term memory.

Poor long and short-term memory are quite often a symptom of incomplete cerebellum development and not a symptom of an "unintelligent brain". Hence the jokes about absent minded professors. It's rather obvious that good memory is important when you're at school, but few realise that certain things that you do with the cerebellum can make a big difference to whether your memory is going to be really good or really poor.

There are several types of memory. Your short-term memory is for the things you are thinking about right now, the plans and decisions you need to make, all this happens in your "thinking brain". Then there's your long-term memory, that's where you store the things that you can recall to your short-term memory when you need them. When you learn something new, it's stored in short-term memory and gets transferred into long-term memory, usually when you sleep. But of course, if your short-term memory is in overload then there's less chance of storing very much until you sleep, hence you retain and learn less.

The more you develop the cerebellum, the more short-term memory space is freed up, the more you can retain until you sleep, the more goes into long-term memory.

A third important type of memory is your "emotional memory", storing the events that happen in your life and the associated feelings that they created for you - whether frightening, painful, pleasant, funny, or sad. These feelings and events are not stored in words in your brain, so the effect they have is in your sub-conscious. They have huge influence on your decision-making and are what can suddenly put you into fight or flight mode without you understanding why.

Children (or adults) that are emotionally highly sensitive show signs of incomplete development of their emotional circuitry. Ironically, the more creative you are, the greater the need for development of brain circuitry.

Forgetfulness.

Ever sent your child upstairs for something and, by the time they get up there they've forgotten what you sent them for? What happened to their memory during the stair-climbing process? The answer may surprise you.

Climbing stairs is a complex balance process, and if it hasn't been made completely automatic, there's a lot of processing going on in the thinking brain to step than falling. In many children, it isn't fully automatic yet so as they take each step the brain is calculating how they maintain their balance and not fall over, how to lift each leg in turn, it's a lot to think about. The processing happening is in the same part of the brain that is storing the list of things you have sent them for. The need for them to not fall over is more important to the brain than the "socks" you sent them to get, so the "socks" gets pushed out of working memory and forgotten. Don't blame your child; they weren't choosing to forget, the space they'd stored it in was needed for something even more important.

Bedwetting.

Approximately one in 10 children that struggle at school have issues with bedwetting long after they should've solved them.

Are they lazy? No. Are they choosing to wet the bed? No. This is evidence of an incomplete process of maturing, and it's neurological. They just aren't sensitive to the need to go to the toilet when they are asleep, and this condition occurs in a few children that are struggling with other learning issues. They all eventually grow out of it of course, but it's very worrying to the parents and embarrassing for the child too.

Itchy labels in clothes.

This symptom took me by surprise. It took me a long time to work this one out, but eventually I realised that a significant proportion of the children that struggled with some aspects of learning found the labels in their clothes dreadfully itchy. They couldn't stand them. They wanted to tear their clothes off just because the labels were itching. And if you've come across this in your child you'll likely have got into the habit of systematically cutting out labels as soon as you buy new clothes, so it avoids the problem. Can you believe that the root cause is linked to the way senses or feelings are processed, this, in turn, has strong connections to the cerebellum?

Travel sickness.

When studying the research data from the many thousands of children I worked with it shocked me to discover that up to one in three children that struggle in school also suffer from travel sickness in their early years. The reason lies in the coordination of sensation and balance in their body. If their brain hasn't fully integrated these feelings, so the brain can work out what is going on then, it can become completely confused when you travel in a car, boat or plane, and travel sickness may be the way it shows its confusion.

Seems deaf - doesn't listen.

This issue causes many arguments in a family. You call your child whilst they are on their computer and say, "Your food is ready", and there's no reaction. Is this bad behaviour? Is your child deaf all of a sudden? What's going on?

If your child has incompletely developed auditory (listening) and concentration processes they have to "think hard" to turn what they hear into something they understand. It may be even worse when they're on a computer or watching a video. They simply don't have the spare mental capacity to do what they are focusing on AND also process what you're saying. The common misunderstanding is that they're choosing not to hear you. Of course, in most cases this isn't true. The absence of processing capacity makes it impossible for them to hear, process, and respond to you at the same time. If you are anything like me, you'll still get furious with them occasionally but at least now you know they are not doing it deliberately.

Picky eating.

We all know that "we are what we eat" and so it concerns many parents that the child doesn't always enjoy the healthy foods that they would like them to have. So they go for fast food. They relish sweet foods and sweet drinks with lots of sugar in and sometimes it's impossible to persuade them to eat healthily. You will be surprised to learn that I have seen significant changes in picky eaters after they have completed a vestibular stimulation course. Some children started to choose better foods and stopped insisting on the unhealthy fast foods that they'd been addicted to before.

Low self-esteem.

Based on my experience with many thousands of children with various learning and developmental issues, I realised at least half of them have low self-esteem. It took me a while to unscramble what was going on in their brain. It seems that when tasks they are doing are automatised to the point that they are effortless, they feel confident and the brain has plenty of happy chemicals flowing through it, self-esteem is high. When the cerebellum has not completed the circuitry to make everyday tasks effortless then what you are doing is mentally much harder, you don't feel confident, you don't have happy chemicals in your brain and self-esteem is lower.

My daughter's self-esteem went up when she did brain stimulating exercises. Maybe your child will have the same experience.

Shyness

Shyness is another confidence issue that can be explained by weakness in neurological development. When a child's communication skills (speaking and listening) are not completely automatised in the brain, the child often develops shyness. The reason is that there is a noticeable delay in the brain's processing time when they are in conversation. The delay can be anything up to a second or more. In a playground, other children have no patience, and will not wait for them to process. This causes confusion and shyness in the child that needs more time when participating in conversations, and they will avoid these situations. This leads to a feeling of shyness when making friends. At least one in four children who struggle with learning suffer from this at some stage of development.

Homework struggles.

Homework is one of the most misunderstood areas in a child's life. It causes arguments, tears, tantrums, and frustration. Very often when a child is struggling to do their homework, it's because it often is impossible for them to do it. In class, they've tried to learn the things they need to know to enable them to do the homework, but they fail to take it in. But the parent expects that the child has learnt AND RETAINED enough in school to do homework easily. If reading is hard, they'll be retaining little if anything. If working memory is in overload then ditto. So, some sympathy is needed here. But have hope, if we can develop the skills that change the fundamentals. I've watched this happen in my stepson in the last couple of years. It felt too good to be true, but it happened before our eyes.

Emotional control, anger, depression, anxiety, panic.

One of the most important discoveries in research in recent years is that development of the balance organs and the cerebellum are critical to having good emotional control - your ability to stay calm and in control at all times.

We all hate the idea of our child being in an uncontrollable state because of overwhelming emotions, so we love the idea of mental strength. Until now we've not realised just how the brain can help us achieve it. How incredible is it that anxiety, panic attacks, depression, anger are all issues which are caused when there is the insufficient development of the neurology that gives us that mental toughness. The balance organ and the cerebellum are highly involved in mental toughness, and we are learning fast how targeted physical exercises can make all the difference to control your emotions. This is truly a paradigm shift.

Phobias.

Yesterday I was talking to a friend who couldn't walk along a pier if there were the slightest gaps between the boards so she could see through to the sea below. This is a phobia that traumatises her. The information her brain is getting from her senses in this situation isn't fully integrated and her brain cannot understand what is happening so gets completely confused. When the brain is confused it feels stress, this can easily turn to panic. In her case, her brain doesn't have a programme wired up to tell it what that particular combination of sensory input means - so she goes straight into "fight or flight". There are many other phobias involving heights, fear of flying, fear of open spaces and so on that are all caused by lack of complete integration of our various senses.

Mental strength is achieved by increasing the coordination of our sensory integration, and can be developed by carefully selected physical exercises. For some this has proven to be an effective solution for phobias.

Trauma in childhood.

There are some very critical ages where specific elements of brain development are happening. When children are traumatised during these specific ages, it can stunt the development of key aspects of their brain and thus affect them for the rest of their lives. It may show itself as a weakness in the ability to learn basic skills or have emotional control. These children are often told that they're less intelligent, stupid or lazy and what effect does that have on them?

Children who've been sexually or physically abused have been shown to develop measurably smaller mental capacities. But struggling children from caring families can also face trauma if their issues are constantly misunderstood. I look back with shame at the time when my daughter was struggling and I didn't understand her. Some of her teachers didn't either, it made no sense that a seemingly bright girl couldn't retain basic knowledge, so she was often treated with impatience and misunderstanding, she was often accused of "not trying" when she was doing her best. As I write this, there are tears in my eyes as I cannot imagine the pain that she went through during those years.

Such misunderstanding causes children huge confusion and trauma and can have a serious impact on development. Children that suffer traumas between the ages of three and four will be affected significantly in the development of their emotional controls. They will tend to be far more anxious and be prone to other mental disorders like depression or panic attacks as a consequence.

Young children need to experience the feeling that home is a completely safe place, with parents that love them and understand them. If instead they constantly see threatening situations, fights and arguments then this will cause them fear and pain, and it will affect them. It can severely impact the development of mental and emotional robustness by developing a fragile "panic button", a highly sensitive emotional state, which can show itself for the rest of their life. Divorce, arguments between parents and constant drama in the family can all have a significant effect.

Low confidence.

It is neurological, not psychological. Why is confidence even important? Well, it makes all the difference to everything we do. It makes the difference between doing something well or doing it badly, enjoying what you're doing or hating it. Low confidence makes a child scared to death of doing some everyday things that other people find effortless. Confidence is itself misunderstood, and people that have low confidence are also misunderstood. A child can lack the confidence to do homework or face meeting a class full of people he's never met before, or be scared of reading out loud in class. Confidence is valuable in almost all situations and, contrary to what most think, is enhanced by neurological development.

The consequences of having low confidence.

Having low confidence in life means that you avoid challenges, be pessimistic and miss out on opportunities. With no confidence you increase the chances of failing. The mental load of tackling something with low confidence means that the chances of failure are heightened.

When you're confident, the brain is giving off positive chemicals including dopamine, giving you a wonderful sense of achievement. With lack of confidence, your brain is flooded with negative chemicals like cortisol which heightens your fear, your worry and stress levels and it becomes a vicious circle.

Low confidence, low quality of life.

Parents of a child that's not confident worry constantly. One of the things we'd love to give our children is confidence. Later in life, with low confidence, you tend to choose inappropriate jobs and sometimes even relationships. You might choose a partner simply because you feel they won't leave you rather than select someone that you actually want to be with. You may take a job that you are sure to cope with easily rather than your dream job. So it can have long term serious term consequences.

There's no doubt that we make far better decisions when we're confident. When you are optimistic and confident, you increase the chance of successfully doing what you're setting out to do. There are two elements to the consequences of confidence. One is the result, you increase the chances of it being a good result. The second consequence is how you feel about yourself. When you're not confident, self-esteem is low; self-belief is low....and that's a horrible place to be.

How can we affect our level of confidence? When the skills you need are not fully developed and automatized to the point that they're effortless, then what you do is mentally very hard work, and your self-esteem will be low. It's only when everything is automatic, and you're feeling on top, you're in the zone, do you actually feel supremely confident.

What is confidence?

There are two fundamental elements to creating confidence. To perform any task or skill well, you need to practise it. The common expression is "Practice makes perfect". Sadly, that isn't always true. Practice makes perfect only if your cerebellum is capable of perfecting that particular type of skill. To perfect it, it means the brain wiring it in a way so that it can perform the task without having to think about it. The role of the cerebellum is to carry out and complete the "learning" or "wiring" for that task so that you become a natural at that particular skill and exude confidence when you perform it.

Low confidence made her a troublesome pupil.

A woman told me recently that her biggest fear as a child was the prospect of reading out loud in class. Years ago it was common practice for teachers to make pupils do this, sadly it happens in some schools to this day. She felt her anxiety go through the roof as her turn to read out loud in class got closer and closer. She developed various distractions to avoid having to do it, she'd fake sickness or be disruptive. She would rather get into trouble and be sent to the head teacher's office than face the pain and embarrassment of trying to read out loud in class.

Reading involves eye tracking, a skill that she didn't have. Thus when she was trying to read, her working memory was full of processing her eye movements so she could take in the words. Just doing that meant her working memory was already in overload. But she also had a problem converting thoughts into the words she wanted to come out of her mouth. That mental process was also not fully developed, so her working memory was needed to deal with that. But her working memory was already in overload. The prospect of combining two different actions, both of which required her to use her precious working memory space was an impossible task. She was aware of this nightmare scenario and it caused her overwhelming anxiety.

She's left school a long time ago, and decided to do a vestibular stimulation programme to get rid of those gremlins. Today she confidently addresses large audiences who never imagine that she was ever scared to death of speaking out in public.

How did your child score?

The more problems often mean the greater the potential. If you ticked a few of those symptoms - it's great news. These symptoms have the same root cause making it a logical start point to address the issues.

Why has nobody told you this?

Our children spend their early life in schools and an education system appropriately led by educationalists. They are very good at understanding the "teaching" process but you can't expect them to have the understanding of how "learning" takes place

They are very good at understanding the "teaching" process but you can't expect them to have the understanding of how learning takes place in a child at the neurological level.

♦ ♦ ♦

Zoe's Story

Before starting Zing Zoe was struggling in school, she felt like she was dropping down levels and couldn't think properly, getting distracted easily. Zoe is now a happier and more confident child who has a 'can do' attitude.

(Emma Dredge, Mother)

CHAPTER 6

10 TIPS : WHAT NOT TO DO AS A PARENT

*"Labels are for filing. Labels are for clothing.
Labels are not for people"*
Martina Navratilova

Lets recap and make sure you know what NOT to do before we move on to what TO do to get started on brain development - that's the next chapter.

1. **Don't be too focused on labels. Instead of trying to get a label that is based on the symptoms, focus on identifying the root cause.**

2. **Don't be jealous of parents with children that have NO struggles - struggles often masks great potential.**

3. **Don't worry so much – when you have finished the book I hope you have more optimism for your child.**

4. **Don't give up hope - helping them through this requires determination and strength - but it is so very worthwhile.**

5. **Don't obsess over exams. Exams show little about a child's real intelligence. The best brains and innovators dropped out of school. Maybe they wouldn't have needed to had they known what you now know about supporting the cerebellum.**

6. **Don't focus so much on the "psychological" - instead focus on the "neurological".**

7. **Don't rely only on advice from other specialists. Be prepared to become your own neurological expert on this critical issue - your child's future depends on it.**

8. **Don't wait before acting.**

9. Don't allow children too much use of computer games.
When children get obsessed with computer games and play for
several hours a day, it flags up a possible addictive nature that
may harm their development. A gaming child might well be
getting very good at the games they play, but they will not be
improving other skills they need in life. Games that involve
movement (and most real sports will) help your child far more
in the short and long-term.

**10: Don't allow children too much use of their
headphones.**

Children that play loud music for extended periods through
headphones train their brain to respond to a narrow range of
sensory inputs. This hampers their learning ability and
potentially their intelligence. Listening to music through
loudspeakers does less harm. This is the subject of some very
recent research, keep a lookout for more on this topic, it's really
important.

◆ ◆ ◆

Amalie's Story

*Amalie is no longer taking medication. I took her off the Concerta slowly
to make sure she could still manage to concentrate in school… she has a
healthy gut and a healthy brain. She can focus, she is able to work longer
and better, she even wanted to get up early to start again on her homework
for a physics report and she got the highest mark she could. Her reading is
very good but she still misses the odd word. I am so please she is finally
wanting to do homework!!*

*Amalie is also able to clean up her room without me helping divide her
room it into zones so she could overlook it – she even did it without being
asked and said it didn't really take that long. She is so much happier and
she is happy to find things out for herself even using google to research things
and she feels more peace in her mind.*

(Stine Norman, Mother)

CHAPTER 7

HOW TO GET STARTED

*"Failure is simply the opportunity to begin again,
this time more intelligently"*
Henry Ford

A re you ready to change your child's future? The first step to help your child is to understand what is going on. Hopefully, this book has provided you with plenty of facts and hints to help you make this part of the process easy. The next step is preparing for a BIG change. Preparing to take charge and action.

You know that most experts and some teachers totally misunderstand your child and you now know that there's a good chance that your child is not lazy, unintelligent, slow or hopeless.

You also now know more about the neurology and skill development than some of the experts who have failed to come up with a real solution so far.

You are probably getting impatient and excited to get started and wonder how you can get your child's brain tested and find the specific exercises they need to finish their brain's development.

Please make clear to your child that you understand them, that they are temporarily wired to be this way and that you now know they are not choosing to be the way they are. It is important that parents, family, friends, teachers all take this on board so that they're not ridiculed nor are they misunderstood any longer this will take some pressure off them.

Here are some options:

1. **Get started with a free brain assessment called Insight.**
The purpose of this is so you can evaluate how your child's brain is developed, what potential is there for further development and what goals you could consider aiming for.
https://www.withzing.com/freeinsight/

2. **Here are some suggestions of coordinative balance exercises, you can get an idea of the type of activities that might well help your child. You can access other free resources if you google it.**
https://youtu.be/3BwWU-eN-dI

Exercises of this type have been shown in research studies to increase the number of brain cells in the cerebellum.

3. **Use a programme that creates a customised course for my child.**
There are a small number of personalised programmes available and as I've mentioned through the book, creating such a course has been my obsession - for my daughter and for the millions of others suffering. What I've shared in this book is the genuine expression of my experience. Everyone's brain is unique so I can't promise or guarantee that you will get the same results if you put your child

through the programme. So if you choose to, please satisfy yourself that it is likely to help. My determination to help is very strong and you'll find that programme comes with a money back guarantee. You've everything to gain and nothing to lose. If you follow the programme fully for 90 days and haven't seen any progress we will give you a full refund. At the time of writing not a single person has complied and failed to notice benefits at the 90 day mark. We must be doing something right!

It is a fully personalised programme to stimulate and support the cerebellum. It starts with a brain assessment that measures current brain performance and capacity. This will show you our estimate of the potential and gives suggested target scores for the key brain skills.

It specifies physical activities that you do twice each day for six months. They take typically 10 minutes each session and form your feedback the intensity of the programme is constantly adjusted to suit the speed of development of each of the key brain areas we support. Each 30 days, your brain will be tested again, and the progress reported to you in charts with explanations.

During this programme, you will be supported by coaches and have access to a community of other parents in a private Facebook group.

book.withzing.com/test

We've seen amazing results with so many children, some of whom had labels given to them prematurely. They'd been labelled before being checked to see if the symptoms could be helped.

I've shared several stories in the book, including ones from my own family. Often, I've made them anonymous to preserve their identity. However many chose to be very open about their results on our Facebook pages.

Why you must catch this early to avoid adult problems.

The earlier you can help a child that is struggling, the better. In the early years of their life, you determine whether or not they'll have a lifetime of weakness in critical connections in the brain, connections between the logical part of the brains and emotional control. Also requiring development are the connections between the brain's executive function (the boss of the brain) and the hippocampus (the librarian for key parts of your memory), this affects your ability to be rational and put things in perspective. The sooner these issues are addressed the less likely it is that there will be long term impact on quality of life.

The risk of future issues.

Under development in the brain seems to contribute to a tendency to become mentally or emotionally fragile. This is linked to an increased risk of addiction. Addiction to alcohol, smoking, recreational drugs or gambling is often linked to incomplete development. If you want your child to go through life in a balanced way where they make good, long-term decisions, (very difficult with a tendency to make short-term decisions), then I recommend that you find a way to stimulate and develop the cerebellum early on.

At least 50% of children that have learning difficulties have an emotional frailty which can show itself as some form of a mental issue later on. Research has shown that a substantial proportion of those that commit suicide have signs of learning difficulties. These are serious considerations, and some might be prepared to accept that, for instance, their child is not going to "read very much", but it may be the tip of the iceberg of issues they will have to deal with during their adult life. No parent wants to live with an increased risk of depression or addiction in their child's future.

When working memory is limited, emotional overload is likely. You can't easily control anger, can't control frustration, you can't rationalise easily. You risk not being able to put things into perspective because there's simply the insufficient mental capacity to do that. This affects decision making; choices are likely to be based on the limited considerations that your mind can accommodate at that time. Those considerations are likely to be the short-term ones that result in instant gratification.

Pulling it all together.

So, there is hope out there, exciting hope. But when our children struggle we've been used to getting the message that we shouldn't expect things to improve much. Many families have proved otherwise, and now we understand more of the science behind the development of those skills that make all the difference to life. Let's worry less about what causes the problem, and focus our energy on giving them the skills, the mental tools and the confidence that will make all the difference.

Some parents point out that their children are struggling so badly that they need to have meds to help them cope. I understand that and meds are sometimes needed to deal with a situation, but meds rarely tackle the root cause. If the cause is neurological, the best solution is neurological. I believe that the clue is in the links between the vestibular symptom and the cerebellum. The work we're doing now is showing really encouraging results. Does it need more work? Yes, and we will continue searching for even more relevant research from around the world to add to the picture that's emerged. But, do families have time to wait and see what happens? No, they want a solution now and the wonderful thing about vestibular stimulation is that there is no downside to it if it's done properly. It's completely natural in that it uses the brain's own resources to create better skills, so it's well worth giving it a chance to show what it can achieve.

◆ ◆ ◆

Mark's Story

I first noticed the benefits in my sport after around two months; seemingly overnight, I went from struggling with certain trickier skills in hockey to being able to perform them comfortably and consistently. From this point on, I found it became far easier to learn new skills in sport, as well as being able to easily manage and stay on top of a busy timetable of school work and training. The changes in my organisation were the most noticeable. Before the programme I was known for being forgetful, often late as a result, as well as lacking punctuality when it came to school work. After the Zing, this completely changed and the improvement was often mentioned to me. I no longer struggled to fit school work between training sessions, matches and other things in life, managing to find a way to fit it all in.

CHAPTER 8

WHAT EXACTLY IS MY PROGRAMME?

Vestibular stimulation programmes have been around for quite a while. Most will do some good, so do look them up on Google. As you can imagine we are more than a little proud of ours too.

I have spent millions of pounds on research and our development team has worked hard to come up with a customised programme that fits the needs of each individual. We've never believed that a "one-size-fits-all" programme will develop all of the potential in anyone.

We've put everything online for convenience so that you can use your smartphone, tablet or desktop and the programme guides you through the whole process. Your child starts with brain assessments, they take about 30 minutes and look like computer games. This is a sophisticated way of measuring the current performance of the brain. Then you will get a chart showing the start point and the targets we suggest for each brain skill. At this point many realise that the assessment has recognised the issues and areas of potential improvement, that's a relief!

The system creates a customised programme based on those measures to suit your child. The exercises are designed to stimulate the vestibular in a way that drives the further development of the cerebellum. So, for 10 minutes, twice each day your child will do these activities. You don't need any equipment or sportswear, do them wherever you want. At the end of each session, you report how easy or hard the exercises were, and the programme calculates the optimum set of exercises for your next session.

This continues for 30 days until your child then goes through the assessment again. Graphs will show what's happened to the brain skill scores during the first month.

As your child makes progress for the duration of the programme, the exercises increase in intensity as they progressively drive the development and maturing of different parts of the cerebellum. At the end of the six-month programme a few with very severe conditions might want to choose a three-month extension programme, but for many, six months is enough to see them develop, use, and continue to strengthen those skills that they have never acquired before.

How long does it take before progress is seen?

Normally within a month or two, but for a few, it can be three or four months before progress is seen. You will see both the neurological results and a summary of your own subjective feedback, and it's great to watch children progress from month to month.

Do the results last?

When you learn to ride a bike, you create skills that last for decades. That "learning" was achieved by actions of the cerebellum, the same area we stimulate.

Is it the same as brain-training?

In the last few years, it's become fashionable to do brain training exercises, and there is no doubt that these are good at exercising the existing circuits you have in the brain, which is fine if that's what you want to achieve. However, if you want to develop new skills and remove the limitations, then we believe that brain-training won't do the job. To achieve lasting change requires stimulation of the vestibular, your balance organ, and you aren't doing that when you are playing a computer game.

Why isn't this mainstream yet?

Our world's education system moves and changes extremely slowly. Far more eloquent people than me have spoken passionately about how our education system needs to change far more rapidly.

If you look at a classroom today, it looks very similar to how it was a hundred years ago. And that's not the fault of teachers; it's the fault of the system. The experts in our school systems are educationalists and psychologists. They do a sterling job. They have been established as influential in education since well before the neurology of what's happening in learning was understood. So there's no blame to be ascribed to them. But now we need a new discipline, and that discipline is about how we can create the ability to "learn" within a child. Education does a great job of filling the bucket, and neurology is the missing piece that helps repair the holes in the bucket, so that what is taught is retained.

What should I tell the school when the teacher gives up on my child?

It's not a surprise that teachers don't understand the process we are describing. They get virtually no training in understanding what causes learning challenges. I've asked many teachers, "How long did your training spend on dealing with learning difficulties?" Some say, "None at all." Some say, "Half a day." How absurd is this? Every class has on average one in four children who struggle in some way or other. These children are often extremely bright and have compensatory strategies. They can mask their challenges. But are they achieving their potential? Absolutely not. I regard the obligations of the school is to develop every aspect of a child's development, academic, social, sporting, practical, mental, etc.

One of the most harmful things that a teacher can do is fail to understand why a child is struggling. If a child is struggling for reasons beyond their control, that child must not be criticised for their failings. They should not be treated as if they're choosing to be naughty, to not read, write, spell, whatever it is. What teachers can do is understand. If a child struggles with taking in information by listening, then find ways of inspiring that child and let them learn by doing. Find what they are good at and give them lots of opportunities to demonstrate it.

Don't force a child to read out loud in class if reading is difficult for them. This is one of the cruellest things that a teacher can do, and fortunately it's become far less popular these days, but still exists in some cultures.

Will this really work for any child?

I've yet to meet a child that is fully developed in every aspect of every skill. We all have potential, the ability to become better at certain types of skill. What happens during life is that we end up avoiding those areas we're not "a natural" at, and we focus on our strengths. Good strategy. It works. But when any skill that we're short of impacts our daily life, and that includes skills like reading, concentrating social skill development, then we should focus on them. It's very difficult to have a full and rewarding life without these basic skills.

If you can't dance or speak publicly, then you can probably have a pretty good life without those skills. So they're less important. But I've met many who go through careers where their progress is hampered because they cannot perform certain functions like public speaking. All of a sudden what had been an inconsequential limitation suddenly becomes a career-threatening one.

Our brain has almost infinite capacity. It's almost irresponsible of us not to develop our own brains to the max. It's certainly the intention of all caring parents that their child reaches his or her full potential. I believe the most efficient way of doing that is developing the very part of the brain that naturally wires up the rest of the brain. It's the brain within the brain. It's the part of the brain that makes skills possible, that eliminates the limitations that we have.

What happens if we do not do anything about it?

If we have a child who's struggling with either reading, social skills, frustration, emotional control, behaviour, moods, and we do nothing about it because we hope that the school will, what's the long-term prospect? So many parents (and I was one of them in the past) assumed that the education authorities and the health authorities would make all the best decisions for my child. They would find what's wrong, and they would take steps to deal with it comprehensively. This, of course, is not the case. As parents we must work out why the child has got limitations, work out what their potential is, and set them on a track that helps them fulfil the development of that potential.

If you could turn back time, what would you do differently?

I don't do regrets, generally, but I do have one enormous regret, and that is that when my children were young, I didn't know what I now know. My behaviour towards them, my understanding of them, and the interventions I would have put them through would have been very, very different. And life for them would have been different to this day. Especially my oldest daughter who struggled so badly at school, it affected her confidence and probably will continue to do so. She does now have a far happier life than anyone thought possible.

I would love to be able to help this research reach more - how can I do that?

Our plans include the formation of a "mum's army" - passionate mums who want to help their children and other families. We love being asked this, do email our support team on info@withzing.com. We have some great training programmes and opportunities, it is so rewarding to transform children's lives.

How is your daughter now?

She's running a small business, and she's a positive, happy person that can read and write and do all those things that she could not do when she left school. So her progress has been enormous. I would still love the chance to go back to when she was young and solve her problems at source then, her life would have been far, far richer for her.

♦ ♦ ♦

Natalia & Natasha's Story

Natalie was meant to be writing an English essay and she read it to us and I genuinely thought she'd copied it from somewhere, or someone had helped her, so I was completely blown over when I found out she'd done it by herself and was actually enjoying it for once. That's when we noticed the first impacts of Zing. Her netball improved and she was able to see gaps that even us on the sidelines couldn't see. She was just making better decisions. Natasha was starting her exam year and from going through Zing she found that she could deal with stress in exam situations better and felt more confident because of it.

(Minoo Osbourne, Mother)

NOTES

SCIENCE BEHIND PERFORMANCE
WITH ZING

I founded Performance withZing in order to enhance human performance through utilising the best research in neuroscience.

The company's team of scientists, educators and business leaders worked for many years to develop and test a programme that enhances brain function, based on cutting-edge research from some of the world's top universities. Performance withZing is the result, and the company has developed several programmes for children, athletes, women and men.

Performance withZing is engaged in ongoing research and development, and users will benefit from our dedication to the continual improvement of the withZing programmes.

Brain Performance Drives Development

The withZing programmes seek to develop your ability to learn new skills quicker such that when the cerebellum is fully functional a person's executive functions should improve. Executive functions include attention, working memory and cognitive flexibility. Improving this area will have a knock-on effect on other aspects of a person's life including social skills, productivity and depression.

Many studies have been done on the impact of executive functions but below is a table from **Diamond (2013)** which summarises its effects:

Aspects of life	The ways in which Executive Functions (EFs) are important to that aspect of life	References:
Mental health	EFs are impaired in many mental disorders, including:	
	- Addictions	Baler and Volkow (2006)
	- Attention deficit hyperactivity (ADHD)	Diamond (2005), Lui and Tannock (2007)
	- Conduct disorder	Fairchild et al. (2009)
	- Depression	Taylor-Tavares et al. (2007)
	- Obsessive compulsive disorder (OCD)	Penadès et al. (2007)
	- Schizophrenia	Barch (2005)
Physical Health	Poorer EFs are associated with obesity, overeating, substance abuse, and poor treatment adherence	Cresioni et al. (2011), Miller et al. (2011), Riggs et al. (2010)
Quality of life	People with better EFs enjoy a better quality of life	Brown and Landgraf (2010), Davis et al. (2010)
School readiness	EFs are more important for school readiness than are IQ or entry-level reading or math	Blair and Razza (2007), Morrison et al. (2010)
School success	EFs predict both math and reading competence throughout the school years	Borella et al. (2010), Duncan et al. (2007), Gathercole et al. (2004)
Job success	Poor EFs lead to poor productivity and difficulty finding and keeping a job	Bailey (2007)
Marital harmony	A partner with poor EFs can be more difficult to get along with, less dependable, and/or more likely to act on impulse	Eakin et al.(2004)
Public safety	Poor EFs lead to social problems (including crime, reckless behaviour, violence, and emotional outbursts)	Broidy et al. (2003), Denson et al. (2011)

Source: Diamond (2013).

Brain - Body Connection: The Key to Lasting Improvements.

The withZing programmes supports the brain-body connection. Using a personalised programme of coordinative exercises which you access through an app, we stimulate the connections in your brain required to perform at your best. Neurological assessments are used to monitor your progress and update you on your changes.

These exercises require difficult and careful movements, but no great physical strength or endurance, for example standing on one leg and moving your head from side to side.

By performing coordinative exercises daily, it stimulates the part of the brain responsible for attention, memory and coordination with the intention of making it more efficient and automatic. If these skills become more automatic, there is less stress on the brain increasing the 'mental resources' available for a range of tasks.

The coordinative exercises stimulate three areas of the balance system, and the repetitive stimulation of these system have been shown in research to be development in a region of the brain called the cerebellum. The cerebellum is a small yet major brain region, at only 10% of the brain's volume it holds 50% of the total neurons.

'The Brain's Brain' - An Overview of the Cerebellum.

The power of withZing lies in recent discoveries about a part of the brain called the cerebellum. Sometimes known as "the brain's brain", the cerebellum is responsible for the automation of fundamental skills. These skills include spatial awareness, language skills and social interaction.

When the automation of basic skills is not fully developed, simple tasks have to be undertaken by the working memory — a part of the brain that is critical for processing information and making executive decisions.

The cerebellum has grown in importance with research into the area increased significantly in the last five years as neuroscientists have realised that it plays a larger role and particularly in cognition – a selection of research papers in support of this are referenced below:

- **Cerebellar brain volume accounts for variance in cognitive performance in older adults.** Michael J. Hogan, et al., (2010)
- **Mechanisms of cerebellar contributions to cognition in humans.** Christian Bellebaum, et al., (2012)

- **Seeking a unified framework for cerebellar function and dysfunction: from circuit operations to cognition.** Egidio D'Angelo and Stefano Casali. (2013)

- **The Cerebellum's Role in Movement and Cognition.** Leonard F. Koziol, et al., (2014)

- **Rapid Evolution of the Cerebellum in Humans and Other Great Apes. Robert A. Barton, and Chris Venditti.** (2014)

- **The Cerebellum, Sensitive Periods, and Autism.** Samuel S-H Wang, et al., (2014)

How does withZing stimulate the brain?

At Performance withZing we have built upon research which demonstrates that the cerebellum can be developed through coordinative exercise and particularly through exercises that stimulate the three areas which form the balance system: 1) the vestibular system, which is located in the inner ear, 2) the visual system, which uses information received through the eyes and 3) the somatosensory system, which uses information received from the muscles and joints.

- **Acute coordinative exercise improves attentional performance in adolescents.** Henning Buddea., et al., (2008)

- **Brain changes associated with postural training in patients with cerebellar degeneration: A voxel-based morphometry study.** Roxana G. Burciu, et al., (2013)

- **Increased Cerebellar Volume and BDNF level following Quadrato Motor Training.** Tal D. Ben-Soussan, et al., (2015)

By stimulating the balance system and providing a challenge to the cerebellum, sensory feedback from the body while performing the exercises will indicate a failure to maintain balance, and this will lead to extensive cerebellar activation in 'error mode'. This activation facilitates brain changes, 'shaking' up existing networks, and allowing the connection of brain regions that were previously not connected. Success in this type of exercise will specifically improve the body's coordination under abnormal conditions but can also prime the brain for a change and break of old habits.

What Evidence is there?

There are numerous research papers published on coordinative exercise developing brain function, however, we have selected two easy to understand studies and provided the summaries below. The first study uses elderly participants, being able to show an increase in cognitive function in this declining generation indicates that an improvement could be made in the general population.

1. **Effectiveness of coordination exercise in improving cognitive function in older adults: a prospective study -** Timothy CY. Kwok, KC Lam, PS Wong, WW Chau,

Kenneth SL. Yuen, KT Ting, Elite WK. Chung, Jessie CY. Li, Florence KY. Ho. (September 2011)

40 participants (3 males, 37 females) mean age of 79yrs.

Methods:

Participants from two centres for the elderly were allocated to practice either an 8-week coordination training (CT) programme or an 8-week towel exercise (TE) programme. The Chinese Dementia Rating Scale (CDRS) was used to measure cognitive functioning of participants among other physical measurements. These assessments were administered before and after the programme.

Results:

The dementia rating scale scores (CDRS) of the co-ordination training (CT) group improved significantly from 114.8 at pre-test to 119.3 after training. The scores of the towel exercise (TE) group also improved from 114.9 at pre-test to 116.9 after training.

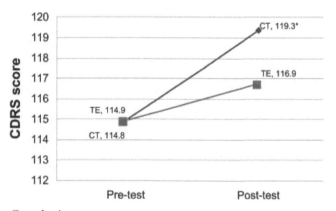

Conclusion:

Findings from this study demonstrated that low-intensity level mind-body exercise could be beneficial to the cognitive functioning of older adults, particularly coordinative exercises.

2. **Acute coordinative exercise improves attentional performance in adolescents.** Henning Buddea, Claudia Voelcker-Rehageb, Sascha Pietraßyk-Kendziorraa, Pedro Ribeiroc, Gunter Tidowa (June 2008)

Healthy adolescents aged 13-16yrs old from an elite performance school; 99 (80 male and 19 female) mean age of 14.98yrs.

Methods:
The group was split into 2 sub-groups. A group of 52 (44 male, 8 female – referenced as the 'NSL' group in the results) who performed normal physical education classes of medium intensity exercise without any specific co-ordinative requests, and a group of 47 (36 male, 11 female – referenced as the 'CE' group in the results) who performed coordinative exercises which were selected from special coordinative training forms for soccer.

The Neuropsychological performance of students were assessed in areas of attention and concentration through an assessment called the d2-test.

Results:
(a)   GZ – total number of responses
(b)   SKL – standardized value of the number of correct responses minus errors of confusion
(c)   F% - number of errors related to the total number of responses

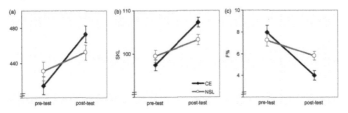

Conclusions:
The results indicate that the group which undertook the coordinative exercises (CE) displayed greater improvements

in the controlled attention and concentration tests over the group which undertook regular physical exercise. in terms of memory, attention and coordination. The Insight assessments used to evaluate user progression are therefore the most accurate in testing performance on these dimensions:

- Memory: long and short term memory recall, working memory (Schoenauer, et al., 2014; Albouy et al., 2015; Moreau & Conway, 2013).

- Attention: task switching and response inhibition (Diamond, 2013; Oei and Pattersen, 2014; Lustig et al., 2007).

- Coordination: motor coordination and timing (Riecker, et al., 2003; and Guenther et al., 1998)

In addition, as a result of these benefits caused by the programme's stimulation, it is reasonable to expect to see beneficial changes in other areas of life and in particular those areas that involve input from the above three dimensions. These can include cognitive aspects, such as enhanced attention and working memory, physical aspects such as game playing and agility, and social aspects, such as better inter-personal skills and confidence. It is therefore clear that Performance withZing can impact not only on learning but also on personal wellbeing.

REFERENCES

1. Bailey (2007)Bailey, C.E. (2007) Cognitive accuracy and intelligent executive function in the brain and in business. Annals of the New York Academy of science, 1118, 112-41.
2. Baler and Volkow (2006)Baler, R.D. and Volkow, N.D. (2006) Drug addiction: the neurology of disrupted self-control. Trends Mol. Med, 12, 559-66. Barch (2005) Barch, D.M. (2005) The cognitive neuroscience of schizophrenia. Annual Review Psychology, 1, 321-53.
3. barton and Venditti, 2014Barton, B.A. and Venditti, C. (2014) Rapid evolution of the cerebellum in humans and other great apes. Current Biology, 24 (20), 2440-2444.
4. Bellebaum et al. 2012Bellebaum, C., Daum, I. and Suchan, B. (2012) Mechanisms of cerebellar contributions to cognition in humans. Cognitive science, 3 (2), 171-184.
5. Ben-Soussan et al. 2015Ben-Soussan, T.D., Piervincenzi, C., Venditti, S., Verdone, L., Caserta, M. and Carducci, F. (2015) Increased cerebellar volume and BDNF level following quadrato motor training. Synapse, 69 (1), 1-6.
6. Blair and Razza (2007)Blair, C., and Razza, R.P. (2007) Relating effortful control, executive function, and false-belief understanding to emerging math and literacy ability in kindergarten. Child development, 78, 647-63. Borella et al. (2010)
7. Borella, E., Carretti, B., and Pelgrina, S. (2010) The specific role of inhibition in reading comprehension in good and poor comprehenders. Journal of learning disabilities, 43, 541-52.
8. Broidy et al. (2003)Broidy, L.M., Nagin, D.S., Tremblay, R.E., Brame, B., Dodge, K.A., and Fergusson, D.E. (2003) Developmental trajectories of childhood disruptive behaviour and adolescent delinquency: a six-site cross-national study. Developmental Psychology, 30, 222-45.
9. Brown and Landgraf (2010)Brown, T.E., and Landgraf, J.M. (2010) Improvements in executive function correlate with enhanced performance and functioning and health-related quality of life: evidence from 2 large, double-blind, randomized, placebo-controlled trials in ADHD. Postgrad. Med. , 122, 42-51.

10. Budde et al. 2008Budde, H., Voelcker-Rehage, C., Pietrabyk-Kendziorra, S., Ribeiro, P. and Tidow, G. (2008) Acute coordinative exercise improves attentional performance in adolescents. Neuroscience Letters, 441 (2), 219-23.

11. Burciu et al. 2013Burciu, R.C., Fritsche, N., Granert, O., Schmitz, L., Sponemann, N., Konczak, J., Theysohn, N., Gerwig, M., van Eimeren, T. and Tinmann, D. (2013) Brain changes associated with postural training in patients with cerebellar degeneration: a voxel-based morphometry study. The journal of neuroscience, 33 (10), 4696-604. Crescioni et al. (2011)

12. Crescioni, A.W., Ehrlinger, J., Alquist, J.L., Conlon, K.E., Baumeister, R.,F., Schatschneider, C., and Dutton, G, R. (2011) High trait self-control predicts positive health behaviours and success in weight loss. Journal of health psychology, 16 (5), 750-9.

13. D'Angelo and Casali, 2013D'Angelo, E. and Casali, S. (2013) Seeking a unified framework for cerebellar function and dysfunction from circuit operations to cognition. Frontiers in Neural Circuits, 6 (116).

14. Davis et al. (2010)Davis, J.C., Tomporowski, PO.D., McDowell, J.E., Austin, B.P., Miller, P.H., Yanasak, N.E., Allison, J.D., and Naglieri, J.A. (2011) Exercise improves executive function and achievement and alters brain activation in overweight children: a randomized, controlled trial. Health psychology, 30 (1), 91-8.

15. Denson et al. (2011)Denson, T.F., Pederson, W.C., Friese, M., Hahm, A., and Roberts, L. (2011) Understanding impulsive aggression: Angry rumination and reduced self-control capacity are mechanisms underlying the provocation-aggression relationship. Personality and Social Psychology Bulletin, 37 (6), 850-862.

16. Diamond (2005) Diamond, A. (2005) Attention-deficit disorder (attention-deficit / hyperactivity disorder without hyperactivity): a neurobiologically and behaviourally distinct disorder from attention-deficit / hyperactivity disorder (with hyperactivity). Dev. Psychology, 17, 807-25.

17. Diamond (2013) Diamond, A. (2013) Executive Functions. Annual Review of Psychology, 64 (64), 135-168.

18. Duncan et al. (2007)Duncan, G.J., Dowsett, C.J., Claessens, A., Magnuson, K., Huston, A.C., Klebanov, P., Pagani, L.S., Feinstein, L., Engel, M., Brooks-Gunn, J., Sexton, H., and Duckworth, K. (2007) School readiness and later achievement. Developmental psychology, 43 (6), 1428-1446. Eakin et al.(2004)

19. Eakin, L., Minde, K., Hechtman, L., Ochs. E., Krane, E., Bouffard, R., Greenfield, B., and Looper, K. (2004) The marital and family functioning of adults with ADHD and their spouses. Journal of attention disorders, 8, 1-10.

20. Fairchild et al. (2009)Fairchild, G., van Goozen, S.H., Strollery, S.J., Aitken, M.R., Savage, J., Moore.S.C. and Goodyer, I.M. (2009) Decision making and executive function in male adolescents with early-onset or adolescence-onset conduct disorder and control subjects. Biol. Psychiatry, 66(2), 162-168.

21. Gathercole et al. (2004)Gathercole, S.E., Pickering, S.J., Knight, C., and Stegmann, Z. (2004) Working memory skills and educational attainment: evidence from National Curriculum assessments at 7 and 14 years of age. Applied cognitive psychology. 18, 1-16.

22. Hogan et al., 2011Hogan, M.J., Staff, R.T., Bunting, B.P., Murray, A.D., Ahearn, T.S., Deary, I.J. and Whalley, (2011). Cerebellar brain volume accounts for variance in cognitive performance in older adults. Cortex, 47 (4), 441-450.

23. Koziol et al., 2014Koziol, L.F., Budduig, D., Andreasen, N., D'Arrigo, S., Bulgheroni, S., Imamizu, H., Ito, M., Manto, M., Marvel, C., Parker, K., Pezzulo, G., Rammani, N., Riva, D., Schmahmann, J., Vandervert, L. and Yamazaki, T. (2014) The cerebellum's role in movement and cognition. Cerebellum, 13 (1), 151-177.

24. Kwok et al. 2011Kwok, T.C., Lam, K.C., Wong, P.S., Chau, W, W., Yuen, K.S., Ting, K.T., Chung, E.W., Li, J.C. and Ho, F.K. (2011) Effectiveness of coordination exercise in improving cognitive function in older adults: a prospective study. Clinical interventions in aging, 6, 261-267. Lui and Tannock (2007)

25. Lui, M. and Tannock, R. (2007. Working memory and inattentive behaviour in a community sample of children. Behav. Brain Funct, 3-12.

26. Miller et al. (2011)Miller, H.V., Barnes, J.C., and Beaver, K.M. (2011) Self-control and health outcomes in a nationally representative sample. Annual journal of health behaviour, 35, 15-27. Morrison et al. (2010)

27. Morrison, F. J., Ponitz, C. C., and McClelland, M. M. (2009). Self-regulation and academic achievement in the transition to school. In S. Calkins & M. Bell (Eds.), Child development at the intersection of emotion and cognition (pp. 203–224). Washington, DC: American Psychological Association.

28. Penades et al. (2007)Penades, R., Catalan, R., Rubia, K., Andres, S., Salamero, M., and Gasto, C. (2007) Impaired response inhibition in obsessive compulsive disorder. Eur. Psychiatry. 22, 404-10.

29. Riggs et al. (2010)Riggs, N.R., Spruijt-Metz, D., Sakuma, K.K., Chou, C.P., and Pentz, M.A. (2010) Executive cognitive function and food intake in children. Journal of nutritional edu. Behaviour, 42, 398-403.

30. Wang, Kloth and Badura, 2014Wang, S.S., Kloth, A.D., and Badura, A. (2014) The cerebellum, sensitive periods, and autism. Neuron, 83 (3), 518-32.